A "Hands On" approach to teaching...

Measurement

PRIMARY

Andy Heidemann

Petti Pfau

Natalie Hernandez

Scott Purdy

Jeanette Lenger

Sharon Rodgers

Ron Long

Linda Sue Brisby

CREATIVE TOYS USA

FORT COLLINS, COLORADO

Primary Layout: Linda Sue Brisby
Cover Art: Petti Pfau and Jeff Barnes
Illustrations: Conda Lou Kane and Linda Sue Brisby

Printed in the United States of America.

10 9 8 7 6 5 4 3

Product Number: 6023
ISBN-13: 978-0-927726-08-5
ISBN-10: 0-927726-08-4

Creative Toys USA
P.O. Box 368
Timnath, CO 80547

Contact us toll free **866-564-8251** or **info@creativetoysusa.com** to become a retail dealer or to locate a dealer near you!

Introduction

This book was compiled by a group of kindergarten through eighth grade teachers at Solvang Elementary School in Solvang, California. It is one of a series of seven books we have written with the purpose of filling a void which we were experiencing at our school, and which we anticipated was being experienced at many other schools as well.

In 1985, the State of California released a document entitled **Mathematics Framework For California Public Schools.** The document was revolutionary in that it sought to restructure the process of teaching math in the classroom. State commitment was so strong that all textbooks submitted for state adoption were initially rejected by the state textbook committee.

Six years later, as we release the second edition of our books, a new state Framework is being readied which re-emphasizes and expands upon the stand taken by the original Framework document. Math strands, domains, manipulatives, problem solving, cooperative learning, and calculators are "IN" (emphasized). Algorithms, memorization, pencil and paper math, and standardized tests are "OUT" (de-emphasized)!

At Solvang School we had been involved in a "hands-on"approach to teaching math for a number of years. Still, we were caught in the situation of wondering how to apply the directions of the original Framework. From this uncertainty came the beginnings of Hands On math books which are an invaluable supplement to your mathematics program.

All lessons described in this book are activity based. We feel strongly that children learn best when they have concrete experiences in learning mathematical concepts.

Our approach is to provide a TASK ANALYSIS of the skills children need to understand MEASUREMENT, and to give a variety of activities which allow children to learn these skills. Activities are organized from basic to complex within each task analysis item and each lesson has a list of necessary materials, recommended classroom organization, and a basic explanation of the lesson format. We have also included extensions of many lessons along with numerous experiences in teaching the metric system.

This book was written BY TEACHERS FOR TEACHERS, and we use these activities in our classrooms every day. All activities involve the use of easily obtainable and inexpensive objects as manipulatives. There is no need to spend large sums of money to teach math. We also feel that this approach enhances the "real world" applications of our lessons. We have left out the typical flow charts, color coding, and cross reference pages that often accompany multi-grade level texts. We have included only practical, teacher based information that you can read once and use.

What we have provided is organized, concise, activity oriented lessons for teaching MEASUREMENT to children in kindergarten, first, and second grades. We're certain your children and you will enjoy these activities.

TASK ANALYSIS

Primary

Time - Calendar	P1. Locates and reads the days of the week on the calendar and is able to read and find given dates and days.	Primary
Time - Calendar	P2. States and orders the months and the number of days in each month.	Primary
Time - Clock	P3. Identifies hour and minute (hands/symbols) on both a standard and digital clock and is able to set time to the hour, half-hour,and quarter hour.	Primary
Money	P4. Identifies a penny, nickel, and dime and states their respective value.	Primary
Money	P5. Counts to a given monetary amount using coins of the same and of mixed denominations.	Primary
Money	P6. Makes change using pennies, nickels, and dimes.	Primary
Perimeter	P7. Develops the concept of perimeter.	Primary
Linear Measure	P8. Estimates and counts units of length and establishes need for standard units of measure.	Primary
Area	P9. Builds and counts the number of square units inside a figure.	Primary
Area	P10. Compares the size and area of various shapes.	Primary
Weight	P11. Weighs and compares the weight of two simple objects using arbitrary units of measure.	Primary
Volume	P12. Uses arbitrary units to make an estimate, and measurement, and an order for the volume of various containers.	Primary
Liquid Measure	P13. Measures amounts in pints, quarts, and gallons.	Primary

Grades 3 - 8

Time - Clock	1. Configures hour and minute hands to five minute settings and counts by fives to sixty.	Middle
Time - Clock	2. Sets clock to writes in conventional notation to one minute intervals.	Middle
Time - Clock	3. States time equivalency and patterns for seconds, minutes, hours, days, weeks, months, years, decades, and centuries.	Middle/Upper
Time - Clock	4. Identifies AM/PM and time zone relationships and purposes.	Upper
Time - Clock	5. Uses a stop watch and can read time to the 10th of a second.	Upper
Money	6. Counts to a monetary value using coins of mixed value.	Middle

Money	7. Makes change using pennies, nickels, dimes, and quarters.	Middle
Money	8. Identifies quarters half-dollars, and dollars, and states their respective and equivalent values.	Middle
Money	9. Identifies and writes value for a given amount using dollar signs and decimal places.	Middle
Money	10. Adds and subtracts (makes change for) money value up to four digits.	Middle
Money	11. Multiplies and divides monetary amounts by whole numbers.	Upper
Linear Measure	12. Compares, estimates, and measures length (height) in inches, feet, yards, and metric measures.	Middle
Perimeter	13. Measures and computes perimeter in standard and in metric units.	Middle
Linear Measure	14. Converts standard measures of inches, feet, and yards into equivalent values.	Middle/Upper
Linear Measure	15. Identifies and measures the parts of a circle (circumference, arc, etc.).	Middle/Upper
Linear Measure	16. Identifies meaning of milli, centi, deci, hecto, kilo, and shows equivalencies.	Middle/Upper
Area	17. Differentiates between area and perimeter.	Middle
Area	18. Determines and uses formulas to measure the area of various shapes.	Upper
Area	19. Develops an understanding of the meaning of "pi" in using formulas to find the area and circumference of a circle.	Upper
Area	20. Computes surface area of solids.	Upper
Weight	21. Identifies ounces, pounds, and tons (grams, kilograms) as standard units of measure and uses them to estimate and compare weights of various objects.	Middle
Weight	22. Identifies equivalencies of weight Including ounces, pounds, and tons (grams and kilograms).	Middle
Volume	23. Identifies the properties of a cube and constructs shapes using cubes.	Middle
Volume	24. Counts number of cubic units in a given figure and constructs figures to find specific volume.	Middle
Volume	25. Differentiates between surface area and volume.	Upper
Volume	26. Computes and identifies properties and formulas to determine the volume of various three dimensional shapes.	Upper
Liquid Measure	27. Estimates the size of various containers and measures equivalent units among cups, pints, quarts, and gallons (liters, milliliters).	Middle/Upper

Table of Contents

CALENDAR QUESTIONS

1. How many days in the week?

2. What day is today?

3. What day was yesterday?

4. What day will be tomorrow?

5. What day is the (a date)?

6. Name the days in the week.

7. How many __(Fridays)__ are in this month?

8. What is the name of this month?

9. What was the name of last month?

10. How many days are in this month?

11. How many weeks in this month?

12. How many weeks are in a year?

13. How many months are in a year?

14. What is the year?

15. What was last year?

16. What will be next year?

17. What is the date today?

18. What was the date yesterday?

19. What will the date be tomorrow?

20. What dates will be on (a given day)?

21. Give a calendar sentence to tell what the date is. "Today is (day), (month), (date), (year).

22. Give a calendar sentence to tell what day was yesterday. "Yesterday was (day), (month), (date), (year).

23. Give a calendar sentence to tell what the date will be tomorrow. "Tomorrow will be (day), (month), (date), (year).

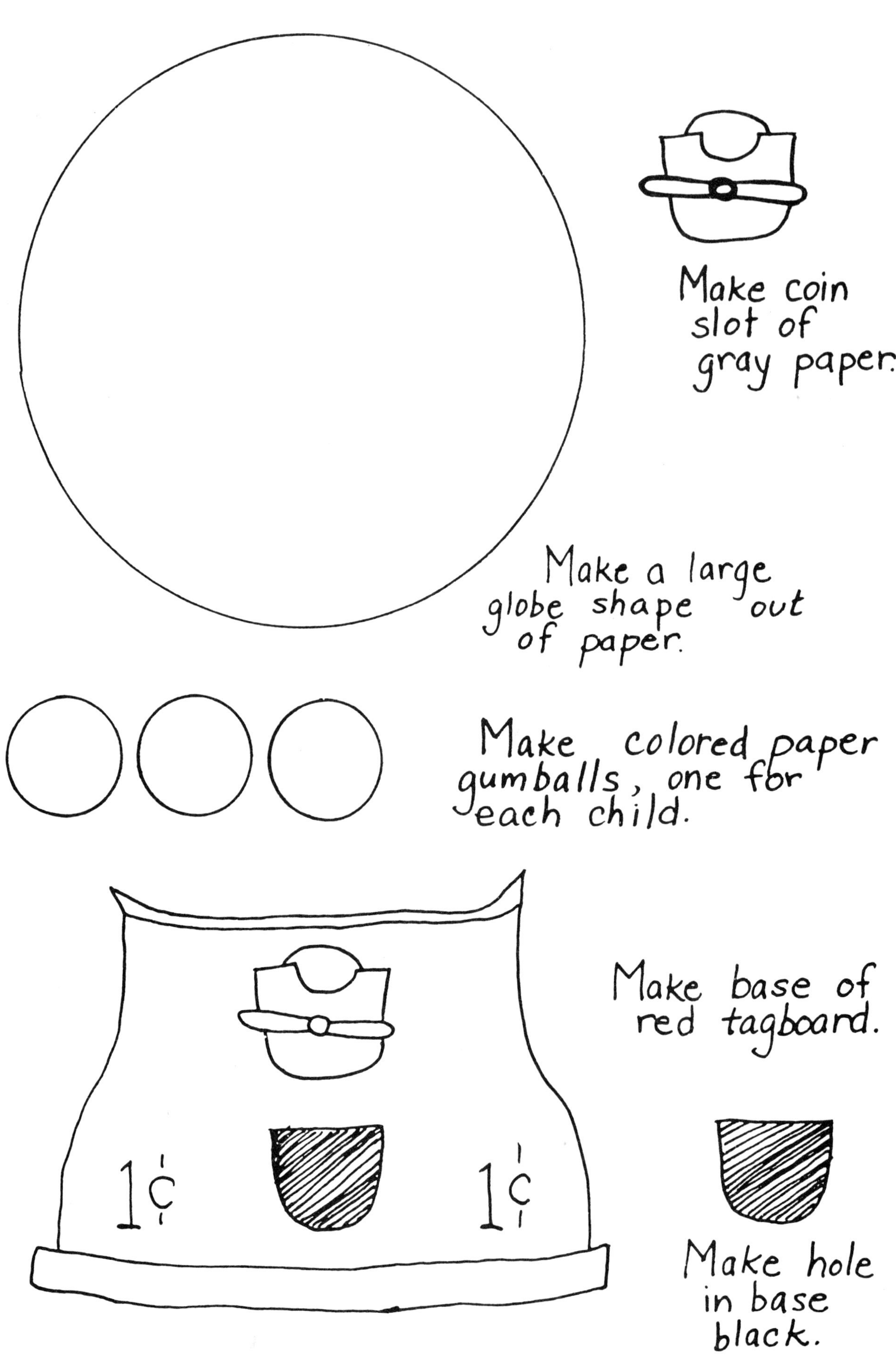
Make coin
slot of
gray paper.
Make a large
globe shape out
of paper.
Make colored paper
gumballs, one for
each child.
1¢
1¢
Make base of
red tagboard.
Make hole
in base
black.

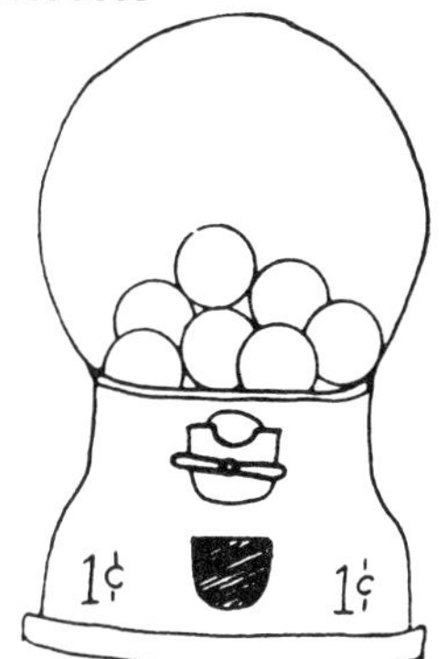

Birthday Gumball Machine

All Year

Grade Level: Primary

TASK ANALYSIS: 1 - Locates and reads the days of the week on the calendar and is able to read and find given days and dates

MATERIALS: Extra-large sheet of red tagboard, large sheet of white drawing paper, marking pen, colored paper gumballs with child's name and birthdate, small pieces of contrasting colored tagboard, construction paper

ORGANIZATION: Whole class activity to be done at the beginning of each month.

PROCEDURE:

- At the beginning of school set up a paper gumball machine to remain in place all year.
- Place laminated gumballs so that the September birthdays are at the top and the August birthdays are at the bottom.
- At the beginning of each month tell children, "We have some birthdays this month."
- The child whose birthday it is removes his gumball from the machine and places it on the correct calendar date.
- Birthday questions to be asked each month are:
- Does anyone have a birthday today?
- How many days until ___________birthday?

  Who can show the day ___________will have his birthday?

  Who can show us the number ______will have his birthday?

  Who can show us the month _______will have his birthday?

  Who can show us the year _______ will have his birthday?
- At the end of each month place the gumballs on the birthday graph.
- At the end of the year read and interpret graph.

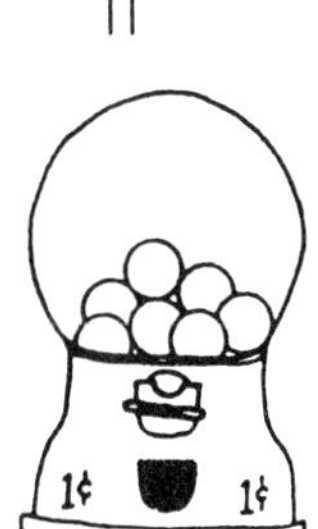

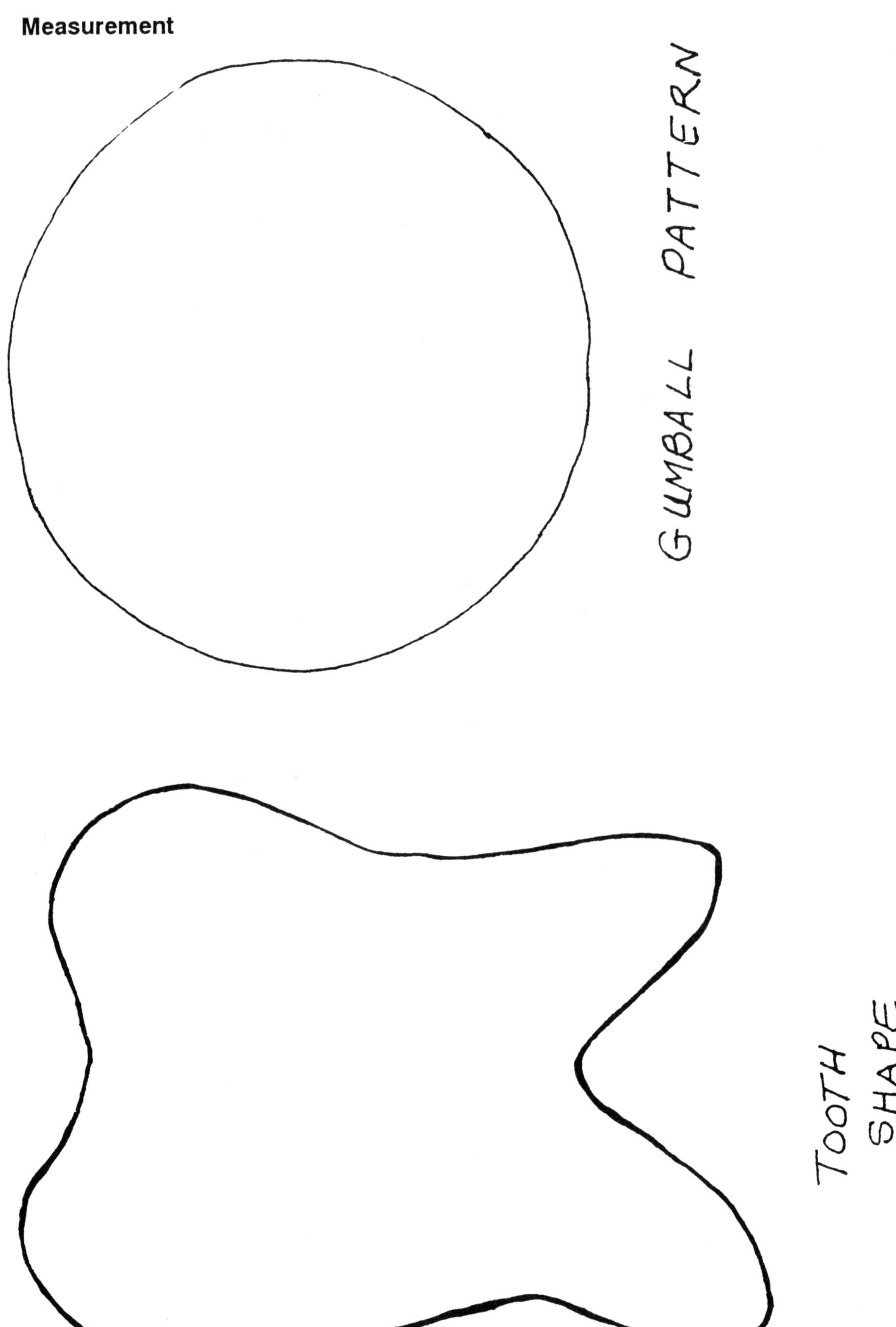
GUMBALL PATTERN
TOOTH
SHAPE

Dino Dinosaur

All Year

Grade Level: Primary

TASK ANALYSIS: 1 - Locates and reads the days of the week on the calendar and is able to read and find given dates and days

MATERIALS: Railroad board, tagboard for at least 10 teeth, marking pen, tempera paint, construction paper, crayons to write names, sponges for painting Dino

ORGANIZATION: Whole group activity: 5 - 10 minutes daily at calendar time.

PROCEDURE:

- Dino should be made and put up before the school year begins; he will not be moved throughout the year.

- Ask children, "Has anyone lost a tooth today?"
- Write child's name on monthly tooth.
- Have child tell a number sentence of how he/she lost the tooth. "I lost two teeth today."
- Ask child to give classmates "toothless" smile.
- Do this daily.
- Each tooth will have the name of the children who lost teeth during that month and number of lost teeth.
- At the end of the school year read and interpret the tooth graph.

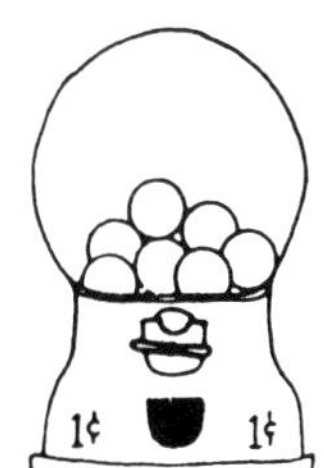

Dino Dinosaur

Construct in Sections of railroad board so it will extend 6 to 7 feet up the classroom wall!

Sponge paint Dino with green and white paint.

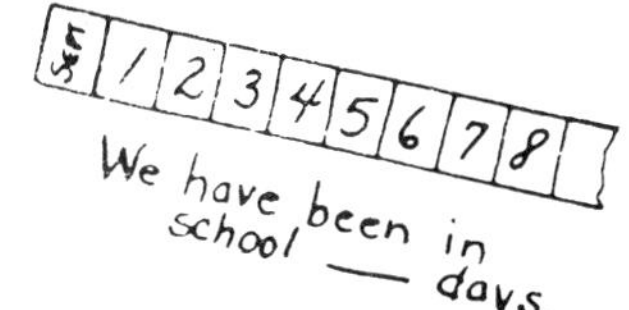

Days in School Number Line

All Year

Grade Level: Primary

TASK ANALYSIS: 1 - Locates and reads the days of the week on the calendar and is able to find given days and dates
2 - States and orders the months and the number of days in each month

MATERIALS: 4" wide strips of white butcher paper in lengths of calendar board (add new length each month), mark off 3" segments, marking pens (red and black)

ORGANIZATION: Whole class activity for daily calendar time.

PROCEDURE:

- First day of school introduce the marked off segments of number line.
- Everyday ask the children, "How many days have we been in school?"
- Have child write number in first segment with black marking pen(teacher may model).
- Count up to each number then ask, "What number comes next?" and "How do we make the numeral?"
- On the tenth day, write the numeral in red.
- Hope that a child asks why the numeral is written in red.
- Ask children if there is anything different about the numeral "10."
- Point out: two digits, zero is one of the digits, zero is an important number because it "holds a place."
- Ask children to give zero a special name.
- Each day zero appears, write the numeral in red (exceptions: 101 - 109).

As number segments are filled, put up in classroom to develop a long number line.
You may use this number line in other calendar lessons with statements such as: Show all the numbers with a "three" in them.
Say the number.
Does anyone see a pattern?
Let's count by tens, fives, etc.

100th Day lessons and activities.
When 100 is introduced, talk about the two places zero holds (ones and tens).
Ask students how they would write a three digit numeral such as 111. Explain why there is no zero needed in this number.
Follow the same procedure for several days.

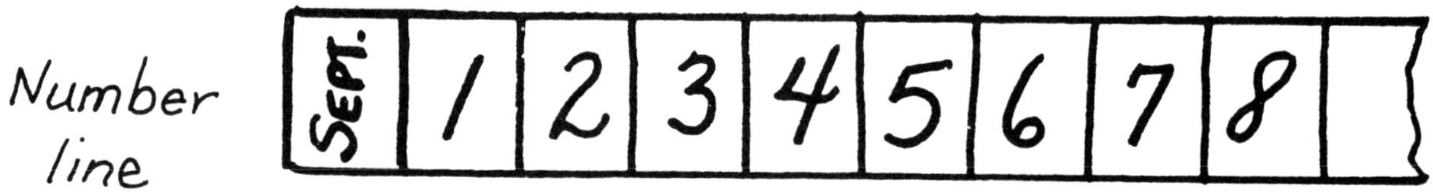

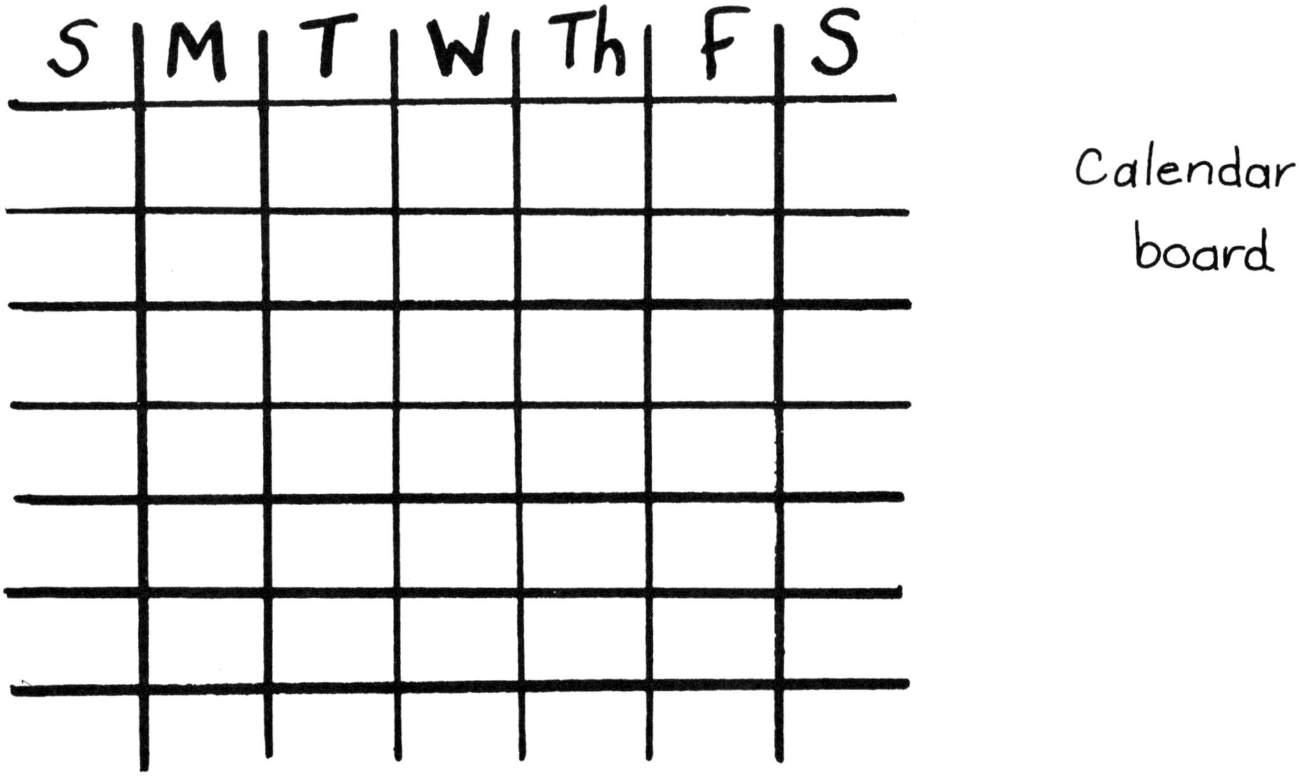

Calendar Math

September

Grade Level: Primary

TASK ANALYSIS: 1 - Locates and reads the days of the week on the calendar and is able to find given days and dates
2 - States and orders the months and the number of days in each month

MATERIALS: Calendar form (store bought lattice or made with yarn or paper), construction paper apples, red butcher paper to make large apple (for tallying number of school days in month), green construction paper for apple leaf, brown construction paper for stem, number line segment (you need a new segment for each month)

ORGANIZATION: Whole class activity
Kindergarten/primary: 20 to 30 minutes of calendar time

PROCEDURE:

- Put up all apples to show children entire month.
- Place birthday gumballs on correct dates and note important days/holidays
- Introduce what a calendar is: days in month, month, days in week, week, date, year, by using "Calendar Questions."
- Teacher and child should show the answers on the calendar.
- Ask children to give calendar sentences or number sentences using daily calendar information.
- Have children chant this information as a group.
- On large apple, child will make a daily tally mark.
- Summarize by having children give a number sentence telling the number of days they have been in school this month.
- In the fall, the teacher needs to model tallying and number sentences.
- Continue calendar lessons with Dino Dinosaur and Birthday Gumball Machine.

September Calendar Pattern

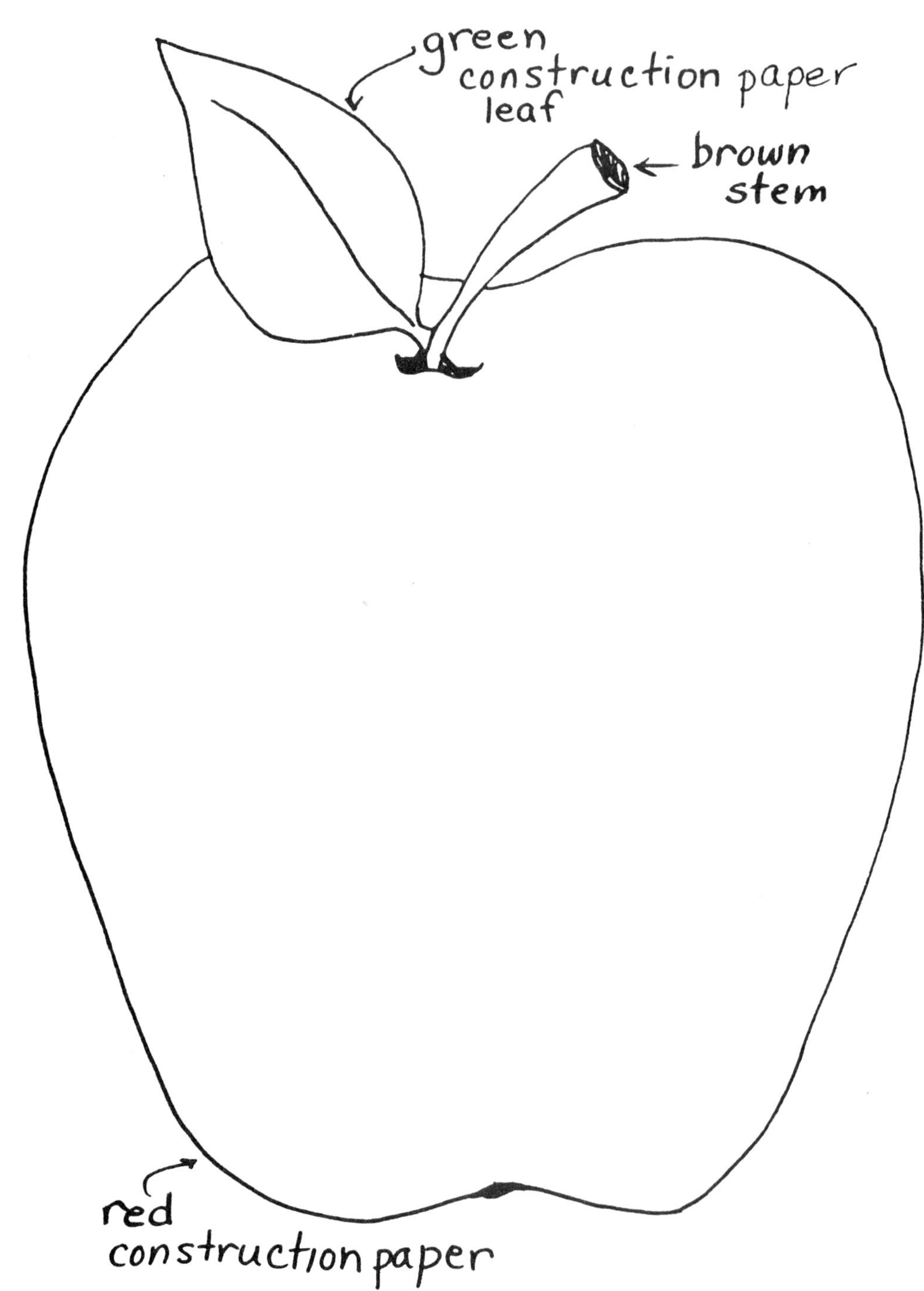

Clancy Clock

Fall

Grade Level: Primary

TASK ANALYSIS: 3 - Identifies hour and minute (hands/symbols) on both a standard and digital clock and is able to set time to the hour, half-hour, and quarter hour

MATERIALS: Large Clancy Clock — large sheet of tagboard, brads, black marking pen

ORGANIZATION: Whole class activity
Kindergarten/primary: 10 minutes of calendar time

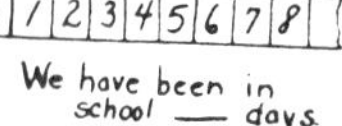

PROCEDURE:

- Make Clancy Clock and display on calendar board (with
- Dino Dinosaur and Gumball Machine).
- Throughout the fall, have students set Clancy Clock to match the classroom clock during calendar time.
- As a reminder for special activities, Clancy Clock may be set to a specific time (i.e. recess, music, P.E.).
- Children are not necessarily "telling time" but are familiarizing themselves with the functions of a clock.

12
1
2
3
4
5
6
7
8
9
10
11
Enlarge
for use on
Calendar board

Minute hand

Hour hand

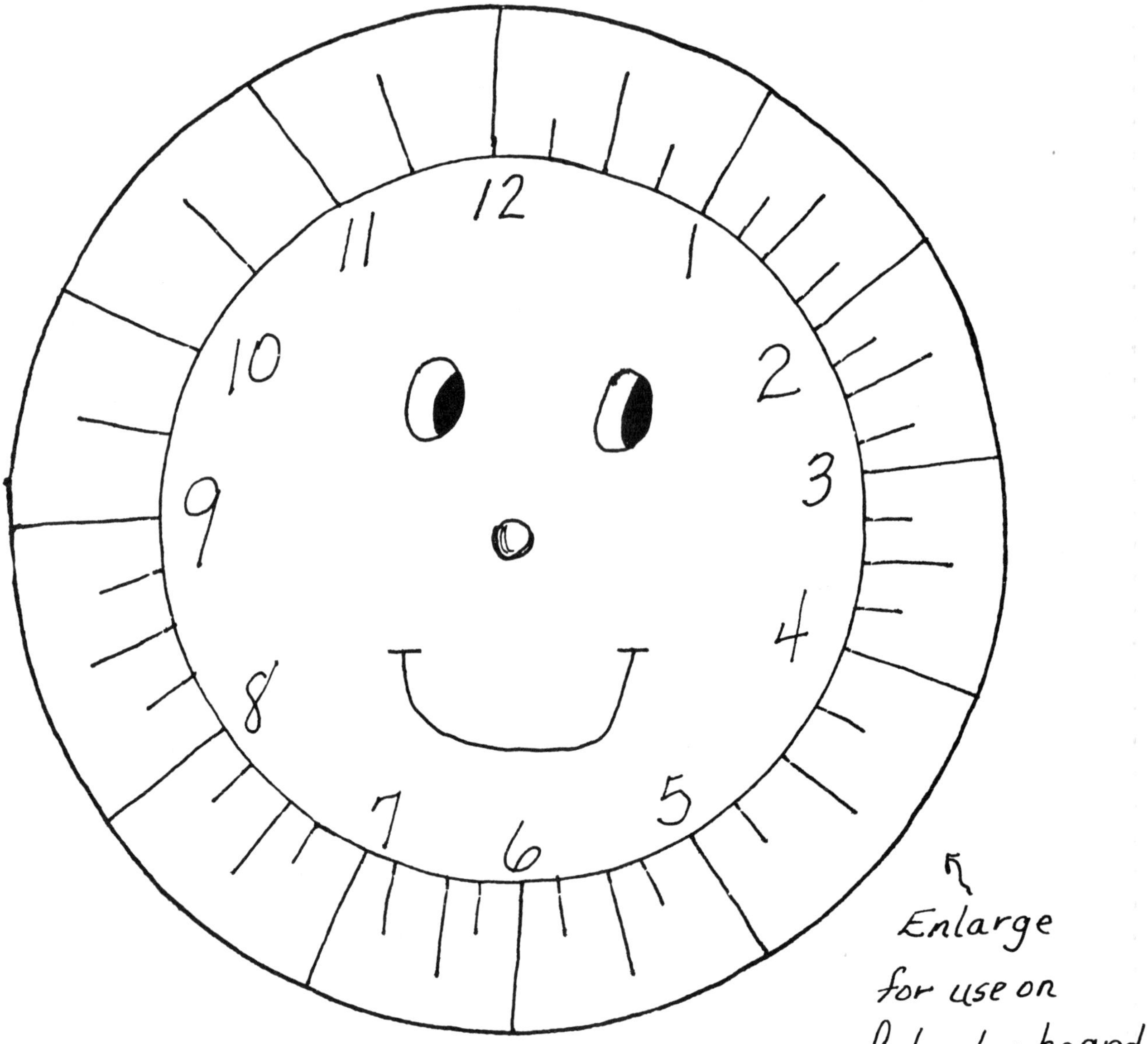

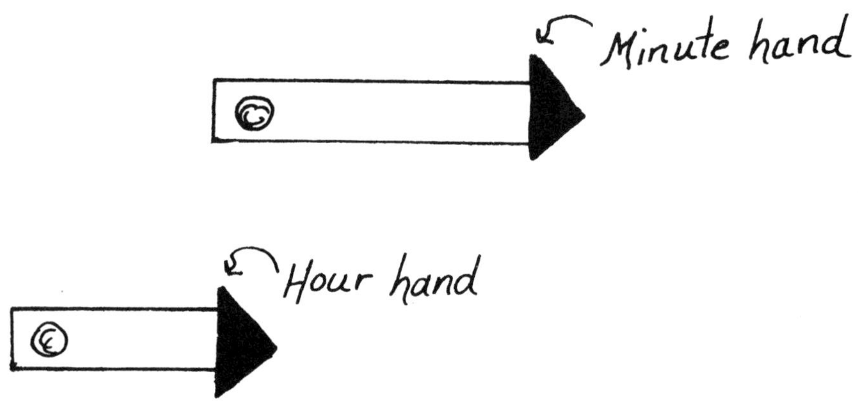

Water, Water, Everywhere!

September

Grade Level: Primary

TASK ANALYSIS: 13 - Measures amounts in pints, quarts, and gallons

MATERIALS: Various sizes of glass jars, water, a safe floor area to eliminate children slipping during water measurement exploration

ORGANIZATION: Cooperative learning groups
Kindergarten/primary: 20 minutes

PROCEDURE:

- Children should be allowed to free explore with unspecified units of liquid measure.
- Have children fill larger jars from smaller jars of liquid.
- Have children estimate and compare liquid measures.
- Pint, quart, and gallon containers should be introduced and used along with other sized jars.
- Have each group give number sentences to describe their liquid measures.

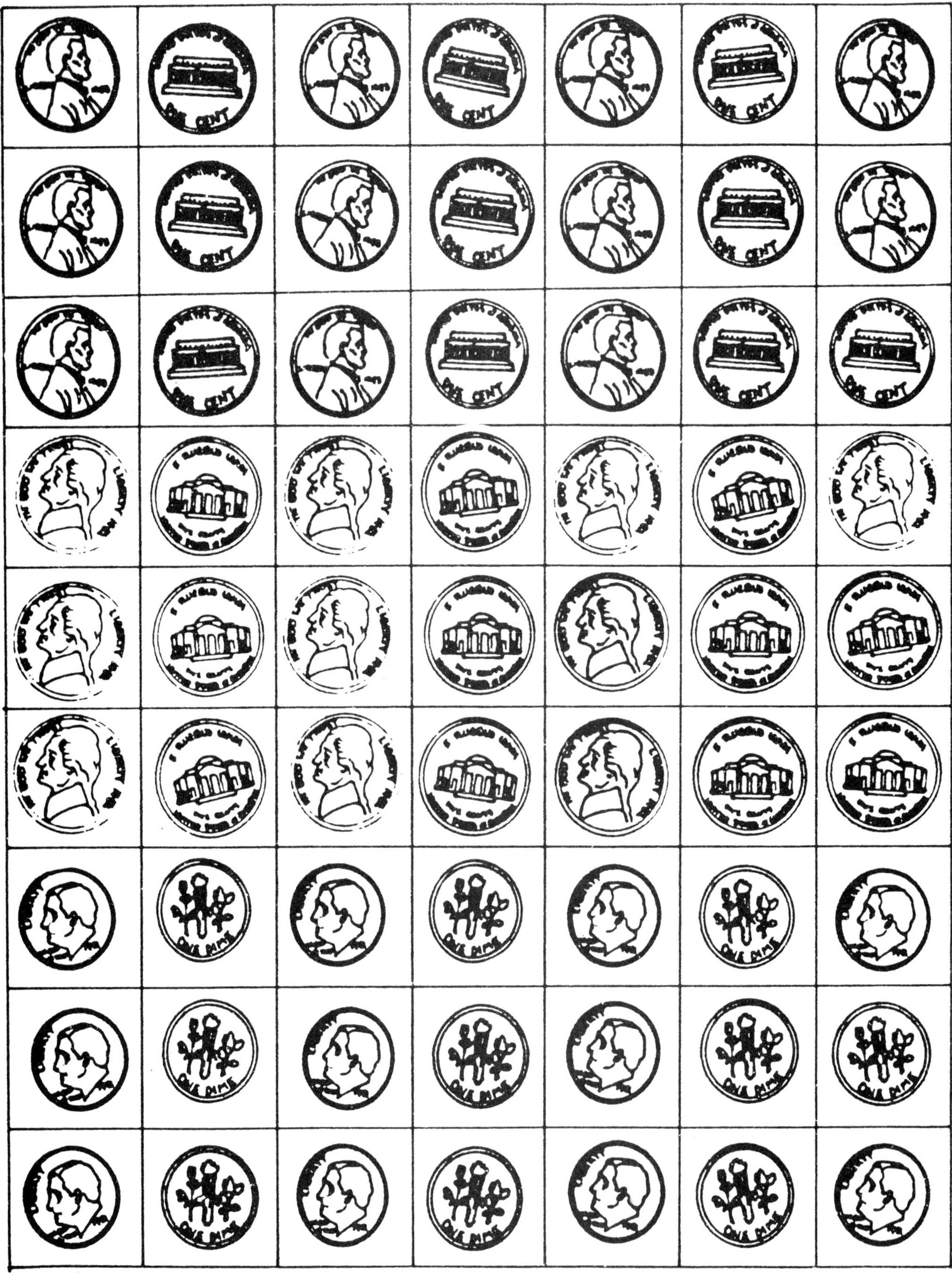

Polly, Nellie, and Dorcus

September

Grade Level: Primary

TASK ANALYSIS: 4 - Identifies a penny, nickel, and dime and states their respective value

MATERIALS: Sheet of coins (pennies, nickels, dimes), scissors, tagboard for masks, brads, string or elastic, Polly Penny, Nellie Nickel, Dorcus Dime patterns

ORGANIZATION: Whole class activity
Kindergarten/primary: 20 - 30 minutes and can be extended to last several days.

PROCEDURE:

- Teacher prepares masks ahead of time.
- Teacher puts on Polly Penny mask and tells a story of the attributes of Polly Penny (looks, value, exchange, size, weight).
- Teacher does the same to introduce Nellie Nickel and Dorcus Dime.
- Next, three children wear masks and ask classmates to bring them coins. For example, "Polly Penny requests 3 cents," and calls on a classmate to bring that amount. This child must bring three pennies to Polly.
- Repeat this procedure with Nellie Nickel and Dorcus Dime.
- Reverse procedure and have unmasked children tell an attribute and take coin to masked child (i.e. This coin is silver and has Monticello on it. It goes to Nellie Nickel).

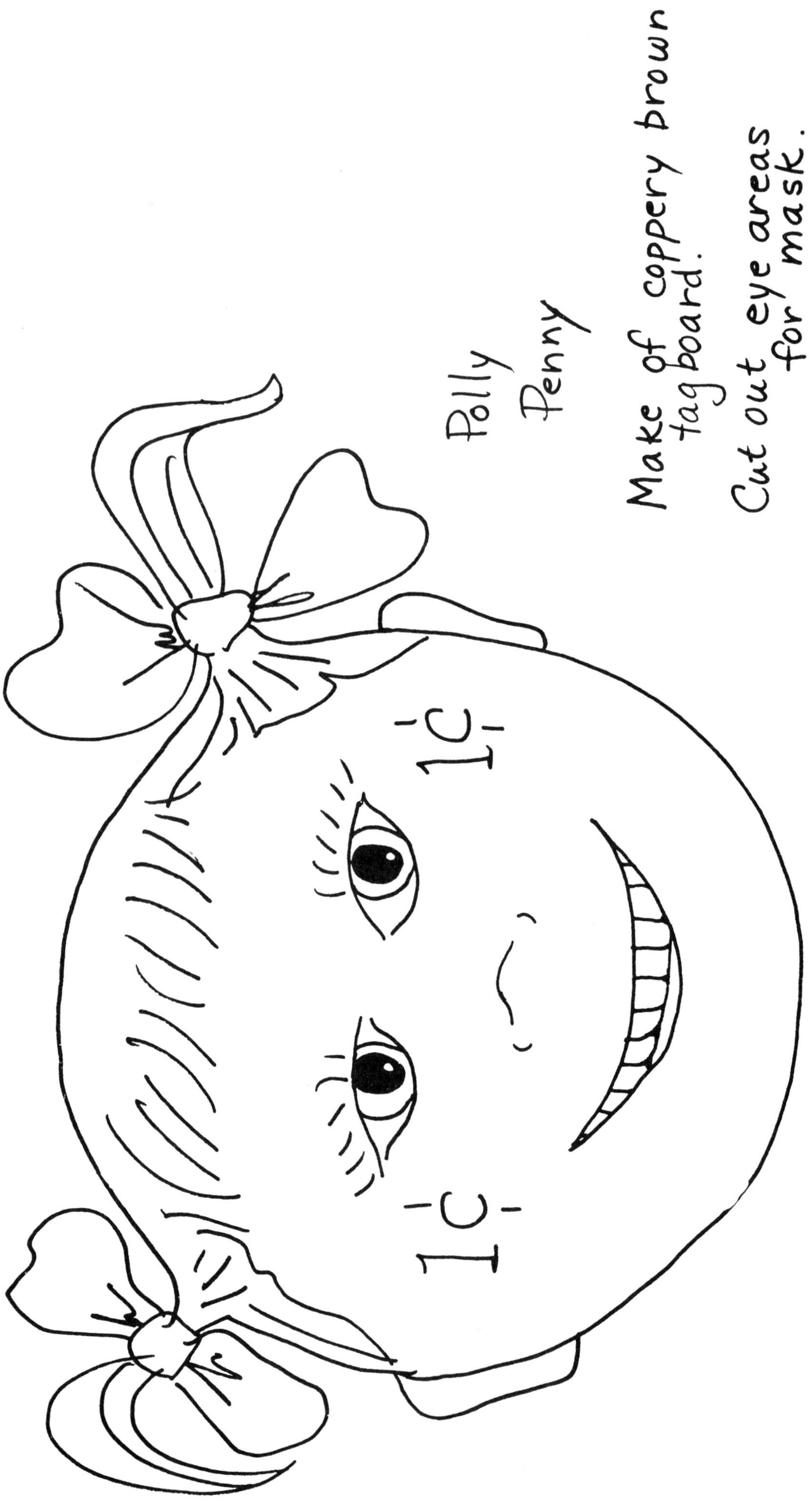
Polly Penny
Make of coppery brown tagboard!
Cut out eye areas for mask.
1¢
1¢

Nellie Nickel

Make of gray tagboard. Cut out eye areas for mask.

5¢ 5¢

Dorcus
Dime

Make of gray tagboard.

Cut out eye areas for mask.

Calendar Math

October

Grade Level: Primary

TASK ANALYSIS: 1 - Locates and reads the days of the week on the calendar and is able to find given days and dates
2 - States and orders the months and the number of days in each month

MATERIALS: Calendar form (store bought lattice or made from paper or yarn), construction paper ghosts and witches hats (to make an AB pattern), orange construction paper for large pumpkin.

ORGANIZATION: Whole class activity
Kindergarten/primary: 15 minutes of calendar time

PROCEDURE:

- Have the month, days, year, birthday gumballs, and special days on calendar at the beginning of the month.

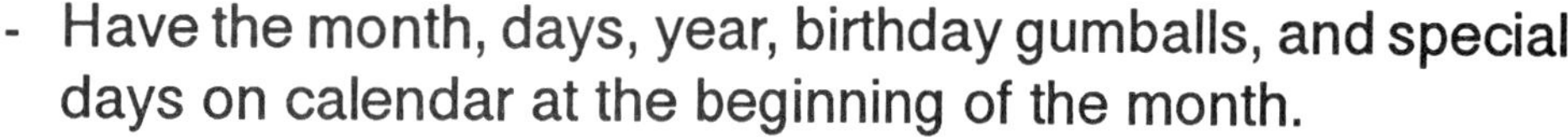

- Put up date (alternate ghost and witch hat on calendar days)
- Put tally marks on large orange pumpkin.
- Ask CALENDAR QUESTIONS daily.

- After a few days (as AB pattern develops) ask children if they see a pattern emerging.
- Ask questions such as: "What does the calendar look like?" and "What will come next?"
- Chant the pattern together.

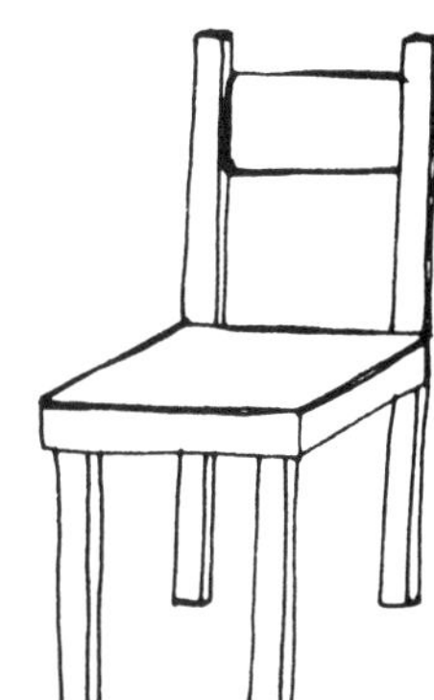

Linear Measure/Perimeter

October

Grade Level: Primary

TASK ANALYSIS: 7 - Develops the concept of perimeter

MATERIALS: Playground, classroom, school structure, student desks, chairs, reading tables, etc.

ORGANIZATION: Whole class activity
Kindergarten/primary: 30 minutes

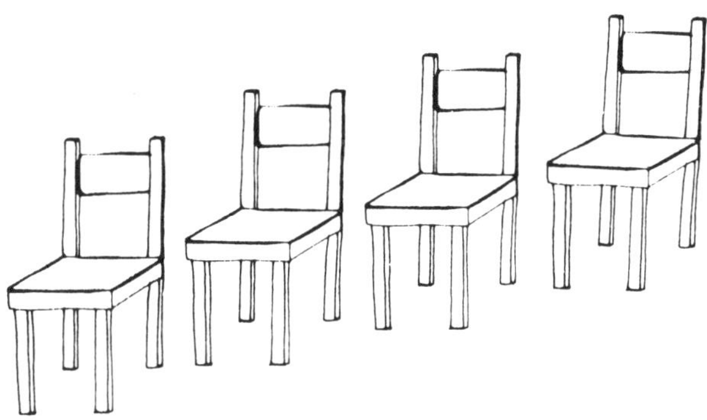

PROCEDURE:

- Teacher needs to prepare children with appropriate math vocabulary: perimeter, boundary, edge, line, measure (tell them that they will be taking a fall walk and will find these things).
- Throughout the walk, dialogue should include statements such as:
- "We are walking around the perimeter of the playground."
- "We are walking on the boundary lines."
- "We are walking along the edge of the school building."
- "We are measuring the row of desks."

- This is merely an exposure to the concept of perimeter and not an exact measuring lesson.

Build and Count

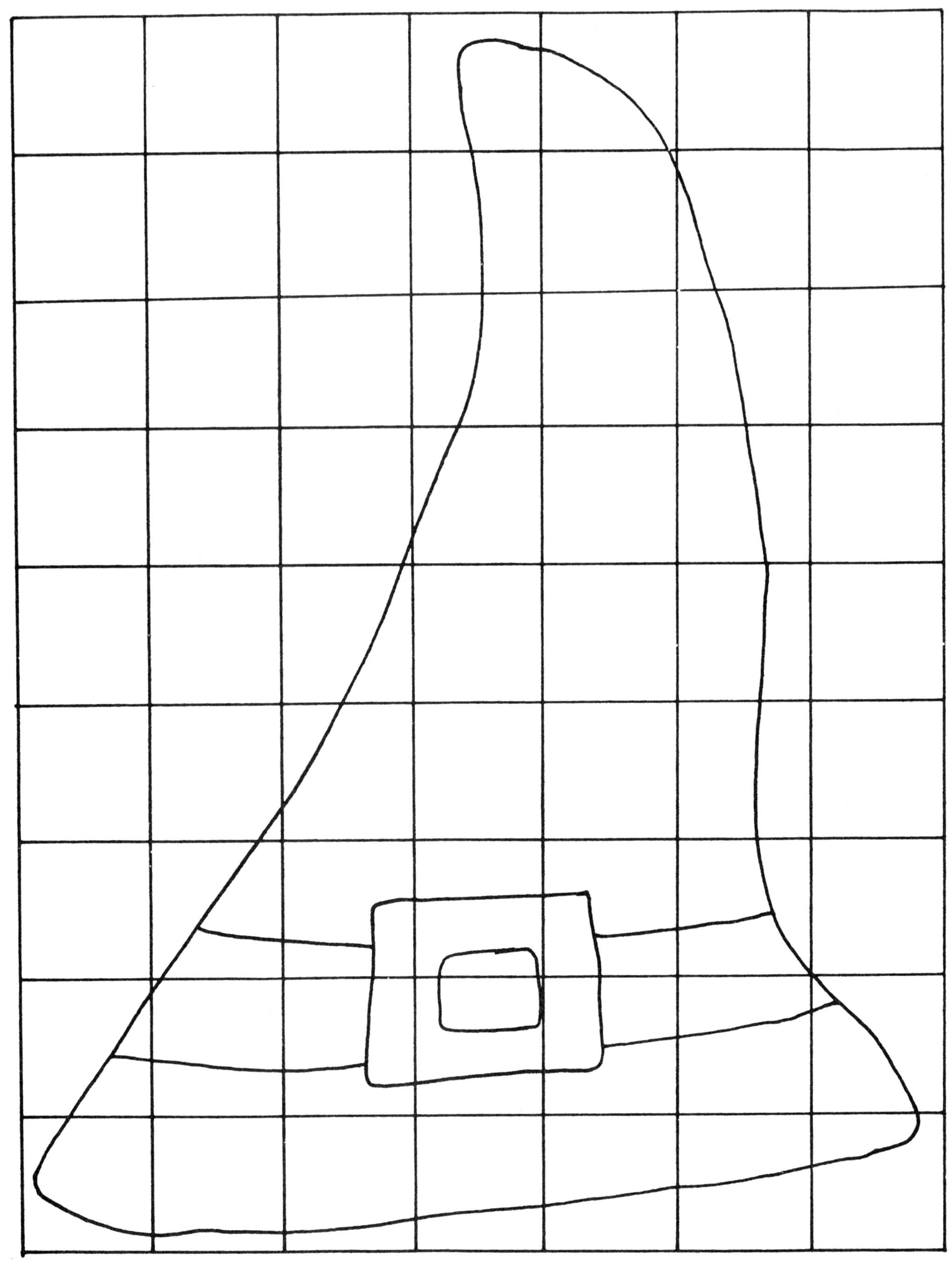

ESTIMATE ____ ACTUAL ____

Build and Count

October

Grade Level: Primary

TASK ANALYSIS: 9 - Builds and counts the number of square units inside a figure

MATERIALS: Xeroxed grid page — one per pair of children, one inch tiles for each pair, xeroxed pattern for each pair

ORGANIZATION: Whole class activity
Kindergarten/primary: 20 - 40 minutes
Cooperative groups of two

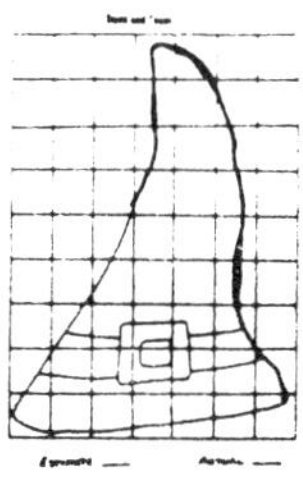

PROCEDURE:

- Give each pair of children a xeroxed pattern, one inch tiles, and grid page.
- Ask group to estimate how many tiles will be needed to cover the pattern.
- Record estimate.
- Have children cover the pattern with tiles.
- Count tiles used and record.
- Compare estimate with actual count.

- Have children decide what they would like to trace onto the grid page — i.e. hand, book, foot, shoe, etc.
- Have children estimate how many tiles will be needed to cover the traced patterns.
- Record estimate.
- Have children cover the pattern with tiles.
- Count, record, and compare estimate with actual count.

How Heavy Is Your Pumpkin?

October
Grade Lever: Primary

TASK ANALYSIS: 11 - Weighs and compares the weight of two simple objects using arbitrary units of measure

MATERIALS: Balance-type scales for each cooperative group, tub of unifix cubes, tub of teddy bear counters, tub of pattern blocks, one miniature pumpkin and one record sheet per cooperative group

ORGANIZATION: Cooperative learning groups
Kindergarten/primary: 20 - 40 minutes

PROCEDURE:
- Each cooperative group places pumpkin in scales.
- Have each group estimate and record the number of items it will take to balance the scales.
- Have each group add items to balance the scale.
- Count the number of items that were needed to balance the scale.
- Ask each group to give a number sentence telling the difference between the estimate and the actual count.

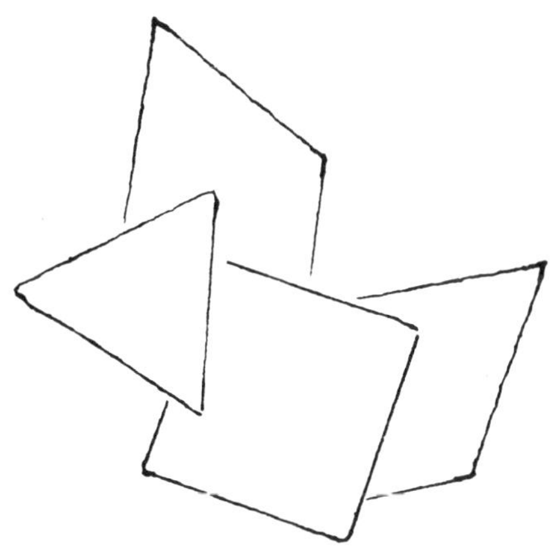

How Heavy Is Your Pumpkin?

ITEM	ESTIMATE	ACTUAL	MORE OR LESS

Whose Pumpkin is Seediest?

October

Grade Level: Primary

TASK ANALYSIS: 12 - Uses arbitrary units to make an estimate, a measurement, and an order for the volume of various containers

MATERIALS: Three various sized pumpkins, carving knives, containers for cleaning and sorting pulp and seeds, butcher paper, marking pens, various sizes of jars for measuring

ORGANIZATION: Cooperative learning groups
Kindergarten/primary: 20 - 40 minutes

PROCEDURE:

- As a whole group predict which pumpkin will have the most seeds and the fewest seeds. Record on butcher paper.
- Divide into cooperative groups.
- Clean out pumpkins.
- Have each group do a second estimate of the size of jar the seeds will fill. Record on butcher paper.
- Have each group measure the seeds, not by counting, but by putting seeds in various containers. Record.
- As a whole class have students line up the filled containers in order of volume (least to greatest/greatest to least).
- Compare and interpret data recorded.

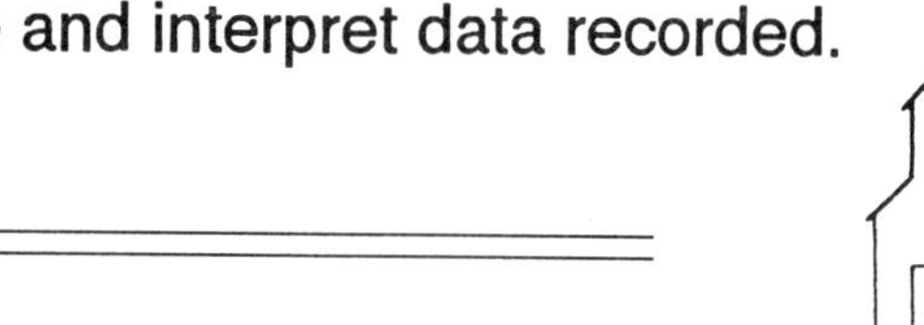

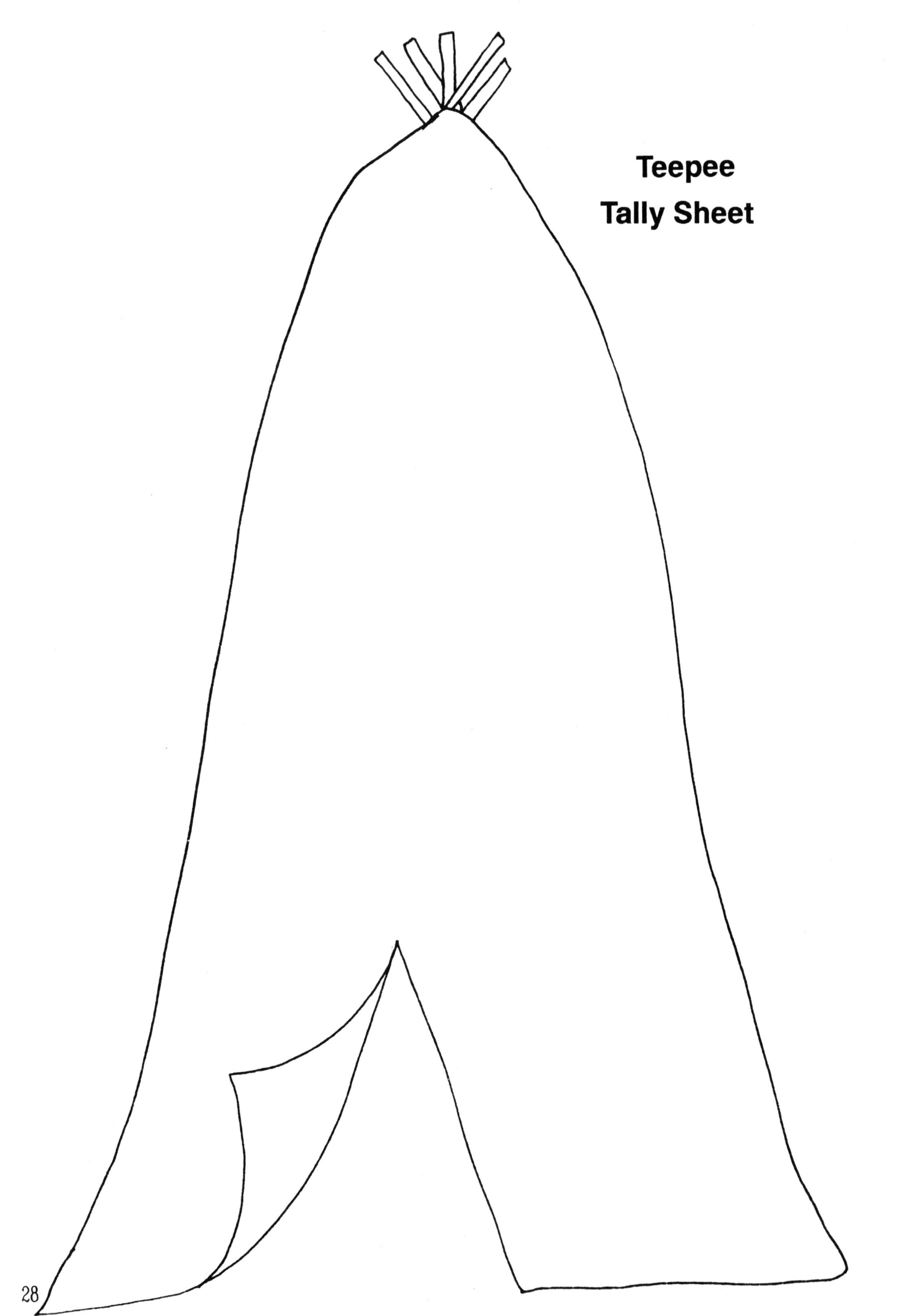
Teepee
Tally Sheet

Calendar Math

November

Grade Level: Primary

TASK ANALYSIS: 1 - Locates and reads the days of the week on the calendar and is able to find given days and dates
2 - States and orders the months and the number of days in each month

MATERIALS: Calendar form (store bought lattice or made from paper or yarn), construction paper pilgrim hats and turkeys (to make an AAB pattern), large construction paper for a tepee

ORGANIZATION: Whole class activity
Kindergarten/primary: 15 minutes of calendar time

PROCEDURE:

- Have the month, days, year, birthday gumballs, and special days on calendar at the beginning of the month.
- Put up date (alternate pilgrim hat, pilgrim hat, turkey) on calendar days
- Put tally marks on large tepee
- Ask CALENDAR QUESTIONS daily.

- After a few days (as AAB pattern develops) ask children if they see a pattern emerging.
- Ask questions such as: "What does the calendar look like?" and "What will come next?"
- Chant the pattern together.

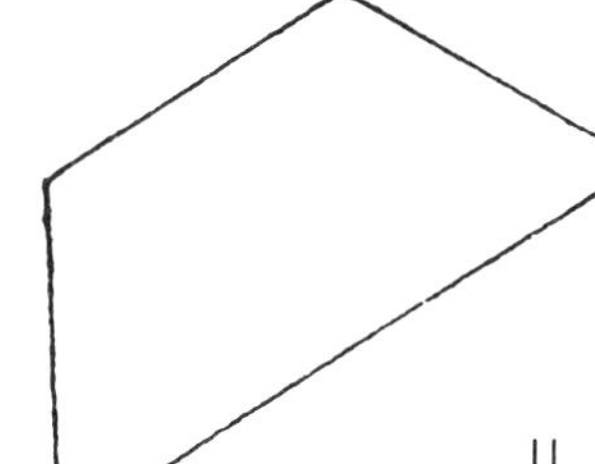

Compare and Exchange

November

Grade Level: Primary

TASK ANALYSIS: 10 - Compares size and area of various shapes

MATERIALS: Xeroxed page of patterns to be used by the children (one per child), one record page per child, pencils, tubs of pattern blocks

ORGANIZATION: Whole class activity
Kindergarten/primary: 20 - 40 minutes

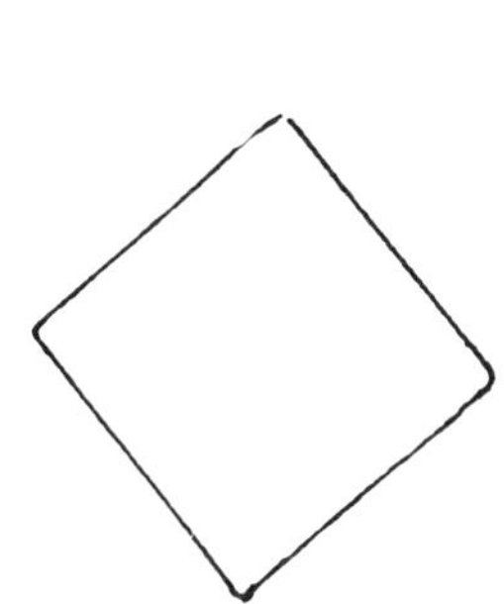

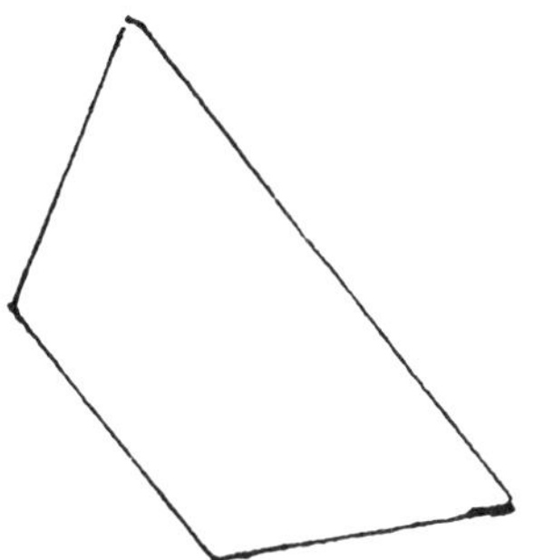

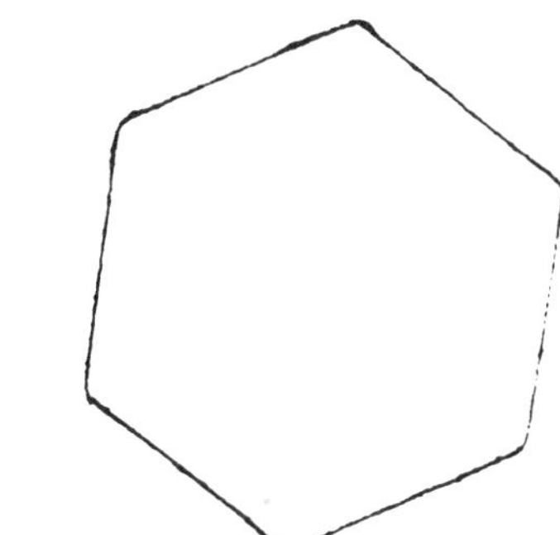

PROCEDURE:

- Give each child xeroxed pattern.
- Have each child cover pattern with one color of pattern blocks and record.
- Next layer, have children use two colors of pattern blocks to cover. Record.
- Third layer, have child use three colors and record.
- Have child compare the layers and interpret by asking the following questions:
- "Using one color, how many blocks were used?"
- "Using two colors, how many blocks were used?~"
- "Using three colors, how many blocks were used?"
- By doing this activity students will begin to see equivalent measures.

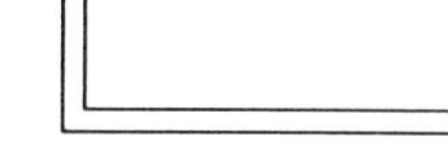

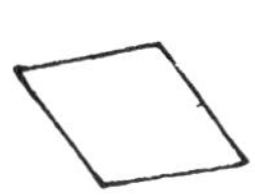

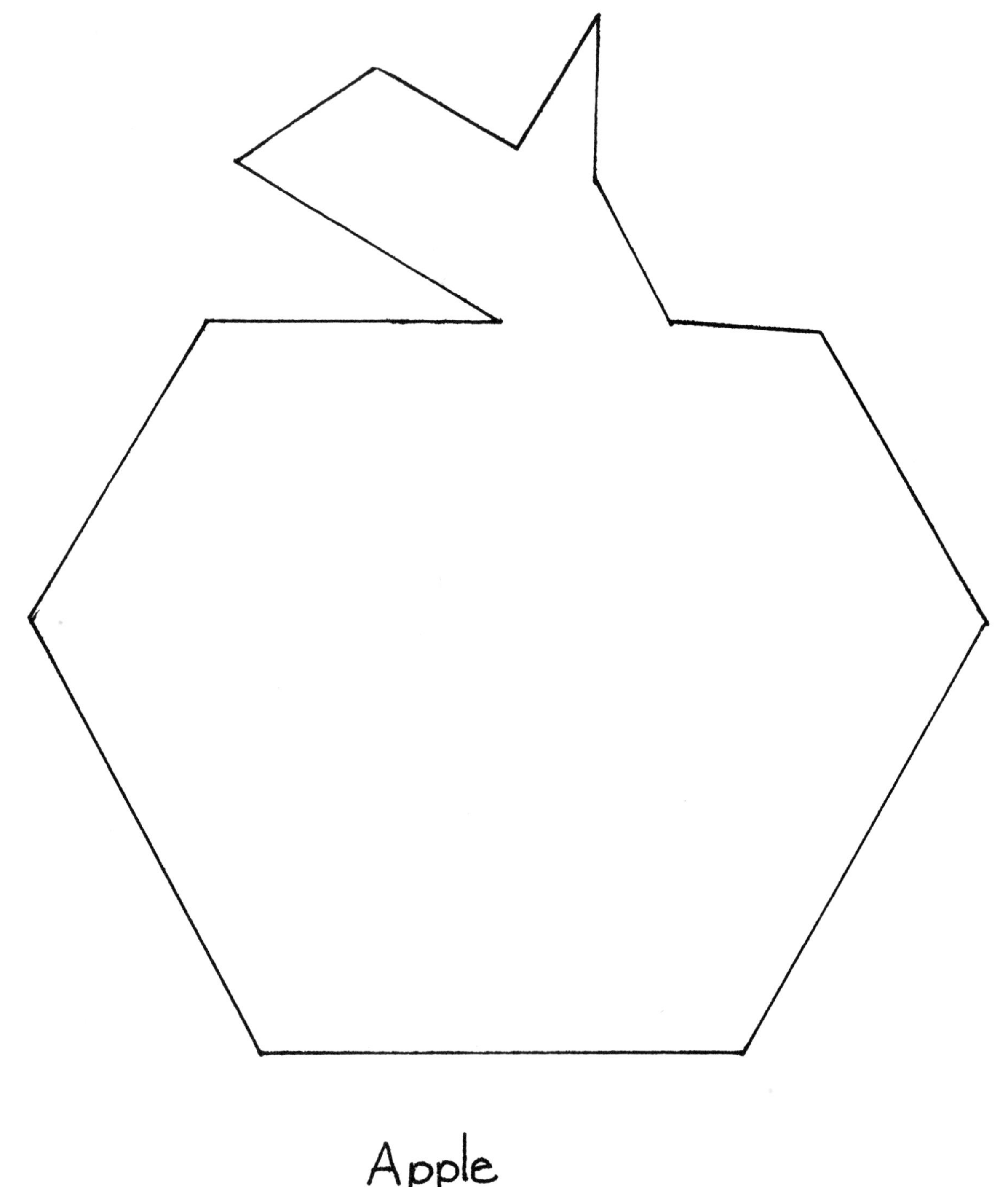

Apple

Compare and Exchange

Pattern	1st Layer	2nd Layer	3rd Layer

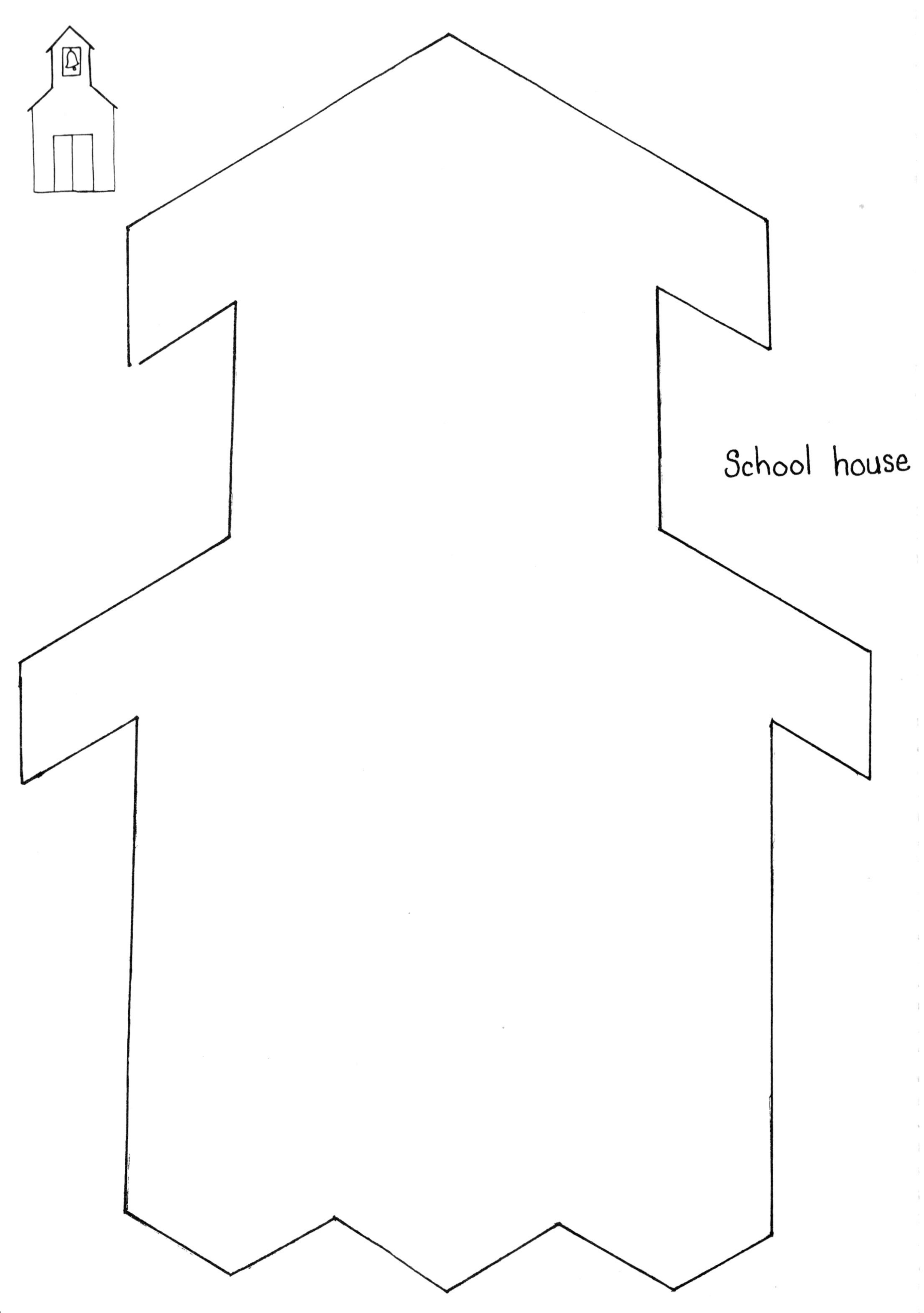
School house

How Much Do Your Ears Weigh?

November

Grade Level: Primary

TASK ANALYSIS: 11 - Weighs and compares the weight of two simple objects using arbitrary units of measure

MATERIALS: Balance-type scales for each cooperative group, tubs of teddy bear counters, pattern blocks, unifix cubes, etc., two miniature ears of corn per cooperative group, xerox copy of record sheet (one per group)

ORGANIZATION: Cooperative learning groups
Kindergarten/primary : 20 - 40 minutes

PROCEDURE:

- Each cooperative group places both ears of corn in balance scale.
- Have each group estimate and record how many tub items will be needed to balance scale.
- Have each group add items to balance the scale.
- Count and record the humber of items that were needed to balance the scale.
- Ask each group to give a number sentence to tell the difference between the estimate and actual count.

How Much Do Your Ears Weigh?

Items	Estimate	Actual	More or Less

Apple Juicy!

November

Grade Level: Primary

TASK ANALYSIS: 13 - Measures amounts in pints, quarts, and gallons

MATERIALS: Various sizes/shapes of glass jars (to include pints, quarts, and gallons), funnels, apple juice (both filtered and unfiltered), ladles, drinking cups, xeroxed sheets of pint, quart, and gallon containers, large sheets of butcher paper, marking pens

ORGANIZATION: Cooperative learning groups
Kindergarten/primary: 20 - 30 minutes

PROCEDURE:
- Discuss the attributes of apple juice (color, taste, texture).
- Compare and discuss the likes and differences of various kinds of apple juice and their containers. Record on butcher paper.
- Questions to be asked:
- "Will the juice taste different?"
- "Will there be more juice in 'this' jar or 'that' jar?"
- "How many pint jars will be needed to fill a quart jar?" (pint to gallon, quart to gallon). Record estimates on butcher paper.
- "How many drinking cups will each pint fill?"
- Give each group of (4 to 6) children a jar of apple juice and the correct number of drinking cups.
- Ask the children to divide the juice equally.
- Drink the juice and enjoy.

EXTENSION:
- Children cut out pint, quart, gallon forms and use them to record estimates and actual measures on butcher paper chart.
- Invite another class for apple juice; determine the amount of apple juice needed to serve the other class.

PINT
PINT
=
QUART

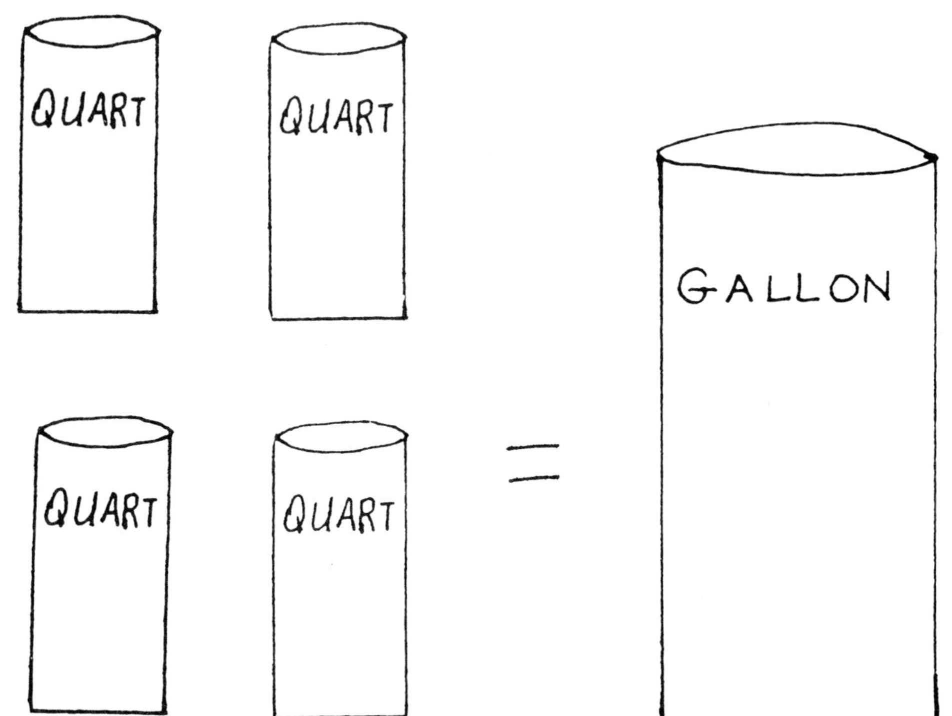
QUART
QUART
QUART
QUART
=
GALLON

Calendar Math

December

Grade Level: Primary

TASK ANALYSIS: 1 - Locates and reads the days of the week on the calendar and is able to find given days and dates
2 - States and orders the months and the number of days in each month

MATERIALS: Calendar form (store bought lattice or made from paper or yarn), 16 construction paper Rudolph and 16 regular reindeer made ahead of time by students or teacher (used for AABB pattern on this month's calendar), large sheet of green construction paper to make evergreen tree

ORGANIZATION: Whole class activity
Kindergarten/primary: 15 minutes of calendar time

PROCEDURE:

- Have the month, days, year, birthday gumballs, and special days on calendar at the beginning of the month.
- Put up date (alternating Rudolph, Rudolph, reindeer, reindeer) on calendar days.
- Put daily tally markers on large evergreen tree.
- Ask CALENDAR QUESTIONS daily.

- After a few days (as AABB pattern develops) ask children if they see a pattern emerging.
- Ask questions such as: "What does the calendar look like?" and "What will come next?"
- Chant the pattern together.
- Ask the question, "What shapes make up the reindeer?" (ovals, circles, triangles, and rectangles).

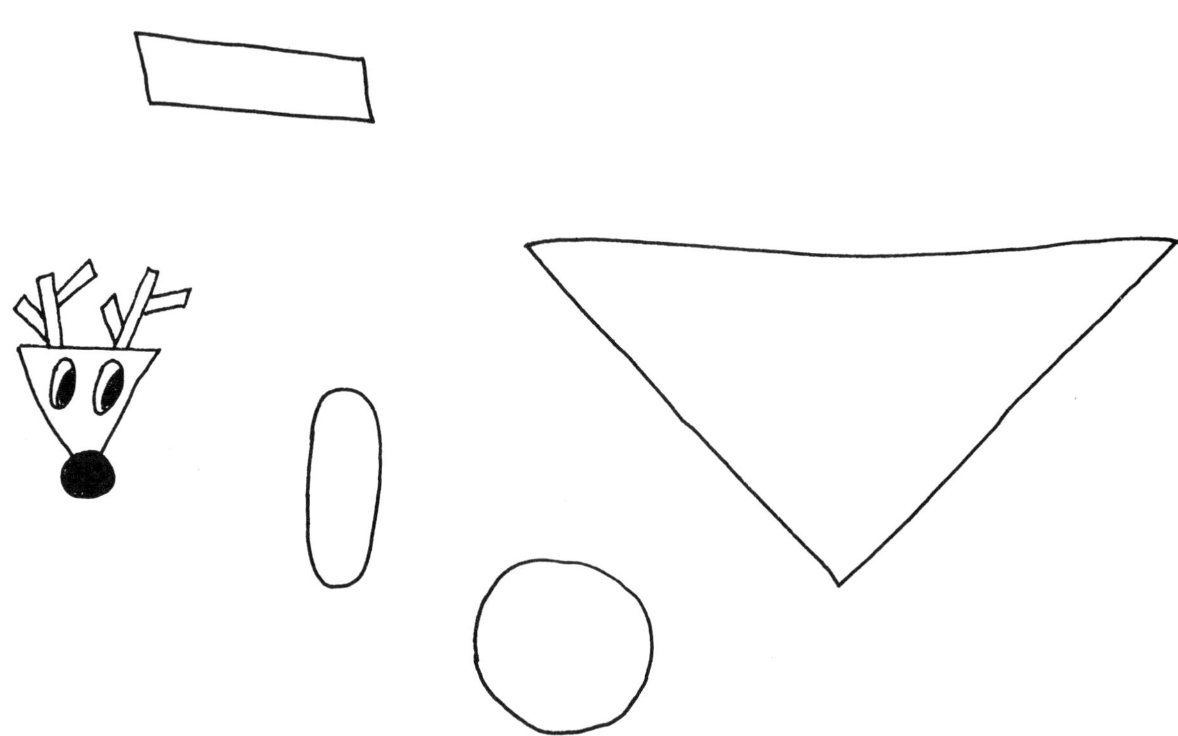

What Is It and What's It Worth?

December

Grade Level: Primary

TASK ANALYSIS: 4 - Identifies penny, nickel, and dime and states their respective value
5 - Counts to a given monetary value using coins of the same and of mixed denominations

MATERIALS: Sheet of coins (page 14), coin masks for Polly Penny, Nellie Nickel, and Dorcus Dime (children make these so they may work in cooperative groups — pages 16, 17, 18)

ORGANIZATION: Whole class activity or cooperative groups
Kindergarten/primary: minimum of 20 minutes

PROCEDURE:

- Give sheet of paper coins to each child to cut out.
- Teacher wears Polly Penny mask and describes Polly's attributes (looks, size, weight, value).
- Same procedure for Nellie Nickel and Dorcus Dime.
- Introduce only one coin per session.
- After teacher has modeled the procedure ask children to wear coin masks and have classmates give attributes of each coin.
- Polly, Nellie, and Dorcus ask classmates to bring like coins to them (penny to Polly, nickel to Nellie, dime to Dorcus).
- When classmates correctly give attributes of coin to masked students, they earn a paper coin of that value.
- Polly, Nellie, and Dorcus ask for mixed amounts (i.e. 27 cents).
- Classmates bring their amounts using all possible coin combinations.

Build and Count

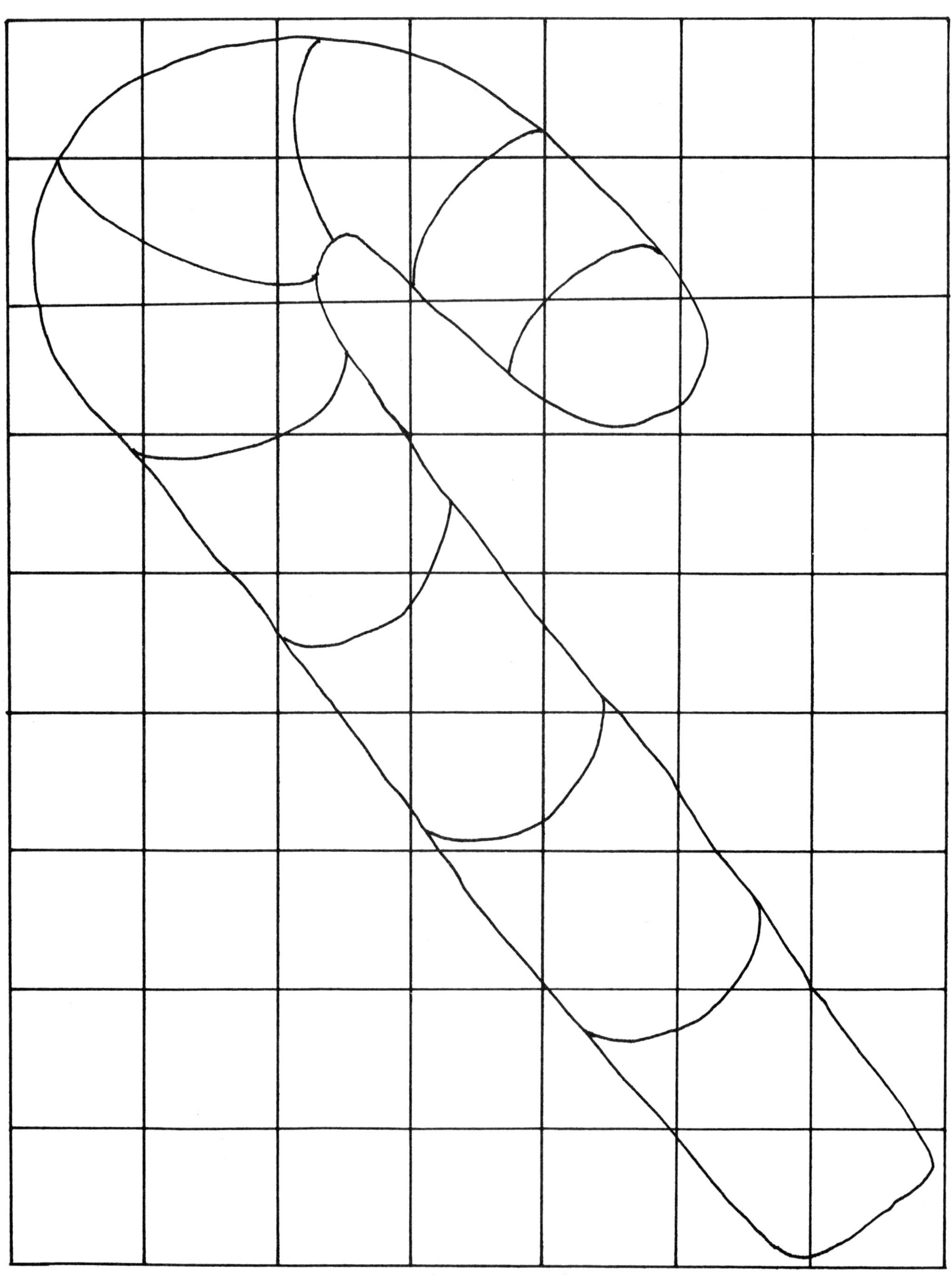

Estimate ______ Actual ______

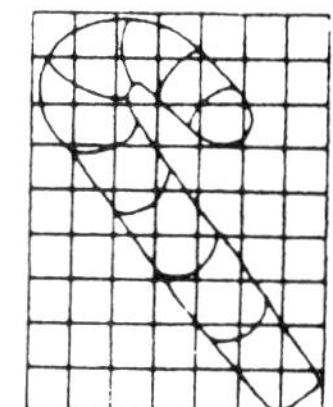

How Square is Your Candy Cane?

December

Grade Level: Primary

TASK ANALYSIS: 9 - Builds and counts the number of square units inside a figure

MATERIALS: Xeroxed grid, page 24 (one per pair of students), one inch tiles, xeroxed pattern (one per pair of students)

ORGANIZATION: Whole class activity with students working in cooperative groups of two
Kindergarten/primary: 20 - 30 minutes

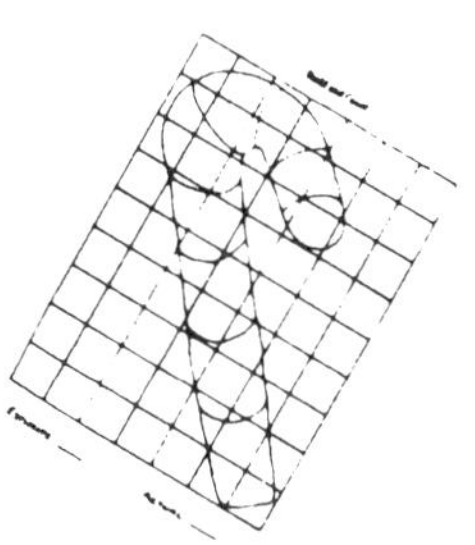

PROCEDURE:

- Give each group a xeroxed pattern, one grid page, and tub of inch tiles.
- Ask groups to estimate the number of tiles it will take to cover the pattern.
- Record estimate.
- Have children cover the pattern with tiles.
- Count and record the number of tiles used.
- Compare estimate and actual count.
- Have children decide what they would like to trace on grid page (glue bottle, chalk eraser, paint cup, milk carton).
- Have children estimate and record the number of tiles needed to cover the pattern.
- Children cover the pattern with tiles.
- Count and record the number of tiles used.
- Compare and discuss estimates and actual count.

How Many Cranberries in Your Bag?

December

Grade Level: Primary

TASK ANALYSIS: 12 - Uses arbitrary units to make an estimate, a measurement, and an order for the volume of various containers

MATERIALS: A bag of cranberries for each group, various sized containers, butcher paper, marking pens

ORGANIZATION: Cooperative learning groups
Kindergarten/primary: 20 - 40 minutes

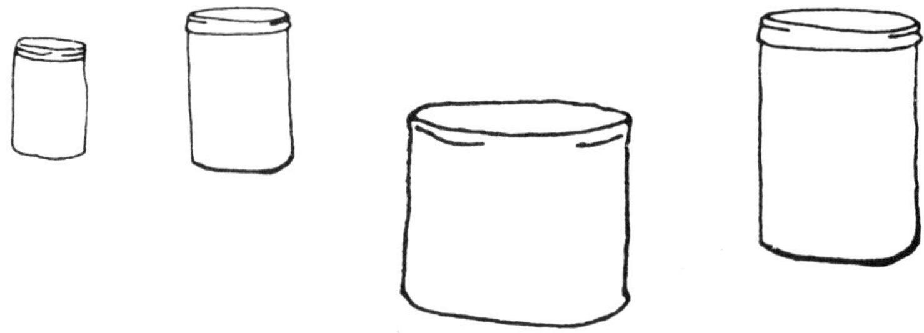

PROCEDURE:

- Divide into cooperative groups.
- Each group predicts and records how many cranberries are in the bag. Record predictions on butcher paper.
- Estimate which containers will hold all the berries. Record.
- Measure using arbitrary units (various sized jars). Record.
- Each group gives a number sentence describing the volume of cranberries in the bag, i.e. "Our bag had one tall jar and two squatty jars of cranberries."
- As a whole class, cooperative groups share their discoveries.

- Berries may be strung for decoration.

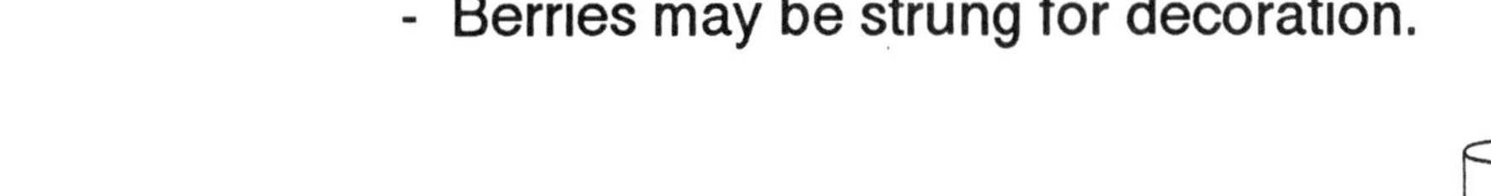

Christmas Party Punch

December

Grade Level: Primary

TASK ANALYSIS: 13 - Measures amounts in pints, quarts, and gallons

MATERIALS: Liquids chosen by the students for their punch recipe, measuring jars (pints, quarts, gallons), drinking cups, ladles, spoons

ORGANIZATION: Cooperative learning groups
Kindergarten/primary: 20 - 30 minutes

PROCEDURE:

- Two or three days prior to the class Christmas party have children do the planning part of this lesson.
- PLANNING:
- Have eeach cooperative group plan one aspect of the
- Christmas party. Include amount of food, recipes (if needed), utensils, and punch.
- After cooperative group meetings have the entire class share group decisions and assign items children need to bring.
- Whole class creates a punch recipe. The teacher should encourage the use of varied (cup, pint, quart) liquid measures.
- PARTY DAY:
- Children work in small cooperative groups to measure the ingredients to make one quart of punch per cooperative group.
- Serve punch for the class party and enjoy!

Calendar Math

January

Grade Level: Primary

TASK ANALYSIS: 1 - Locates and reads the days of the week on the calendar and is able to find given days and dates
2 - States and orders the months and the number of days in each month

MATERIALS: Calendar form (store bought lattice or made from paper or yarn), construction paper circles (8 small with faces drawn on, 8 medium, and 8 large), black construction paper for 8 stovepipe hats (used for an ABCD pattern), one large snowman with scarf and hat.

ORGANIZATION: Whole class activity
Kindergarten/primary: 15 minutes of calendar time

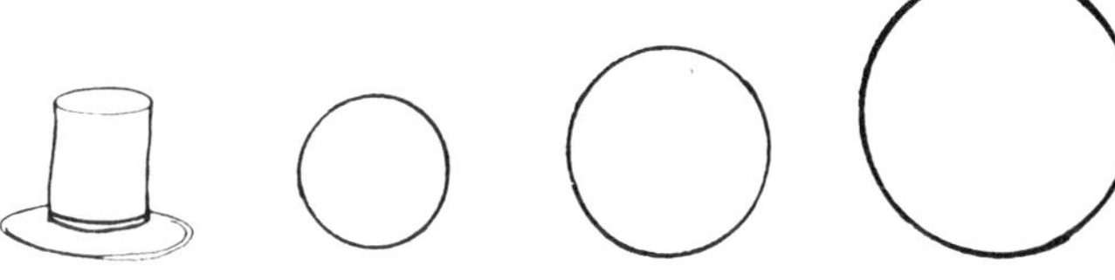

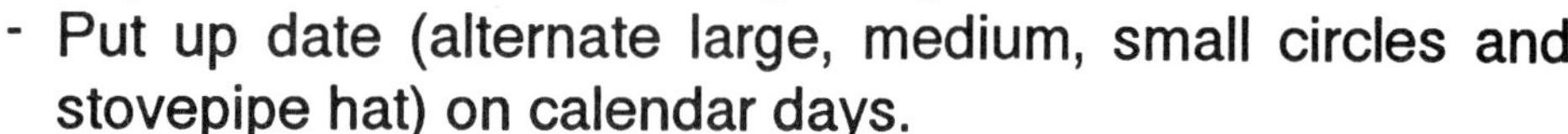

PROCEDURE:

- Have the month, days, year birthday gumballs, and special days on calendar at the beginning of the month.
- Put up date (alternate large, medium, small circles and stovepipe hat) on calendar days.
- Put daily tally mark on large snowman.
- After a few days (as ABCD pattern develops) ask children if they see a pattern emerging ("broken up" snowman should be developing)
- Have children estimate the number of snowmen that will be made.
- Ask questios such as: "What does the calendar look like?" and "What will come next?"
- Chant the pattern together.

12
11
10
9
8
7
6
5
4
3
2
1
LSB

Tick Tock Clancy Clock

January

Grade Level: Primary

TASK ANALYSIS: 3 - Identifies hour and minute (hands/symbols) on both a standard and digital clock and is able to set time to the hour, half-hour, and quarter hour

MATERIALS: Large Clancy Clock and materials for students to make their own desk size clocks (xerox sheet for each child), a large digital clock, scissors, brads, marking pens

ORGANIZATION: Whole class activity
Kindergarten/primary: 10 minutes of calendar time

PROCEDURE:

- Have children make desk top Clancy Clocks.
- Ask a student to help Clancy show what time the classroom clock shows.
- Ask other children to match their clock to Clancy at the calendar board.
- Ask questions such as:
  "What numeral is Clancy's long hand showing?"
  "What numeral is Clancy's short hand showing?"
  "What time is Clancy showing us?" (eight fifteen, fifteen after eight, quarter past eight)
  "What time is the digital clock showing?"
- Teacher needs to do this lesson at appropriate times so childdren have multiple experiences in telling hour, half-hour, and quarter hour.

How Heavy Is Your Heart?

Items	Estimate	Actual	More or Less

Playground Perimeter

January

Grade Level: Primary

TASK ANALYSIS: 8 - Estimates and counts units of length and establishes need for standard units of measure

MATERIALS: Playground, various units of measure (unifix cubes, paper clips, people, shoes, chairs, etc.), butcher paper, marking pens, and masking tape

ORGANIZATION: Small group activity (6-8 children)
Kindergarten/primary: minimum 20 minutes

PROCEDURE:

- Explain to children that they are going outside to measure the perimeter of the playground.
- Ask children, "With what can we measure the permeter?"
- Brainstorm for ideas.
- Choose one item and have children estimate the number it will take to measure the perimeter.
- Record estimates on butcher paper.
- Have children use the unit chosen to measure the perimeter.
- Count the number of units used (or needed) and record actual count on butcher paper.
- Repeat this procedure using different units of measure.

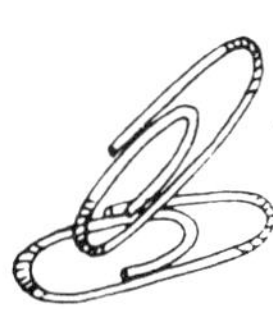

- Upon returning to the classroom follow the same procedure and have children measure desks, chairs, etc.
- Record all data on chart.
- Compare and discuss need for standard unit of measure.

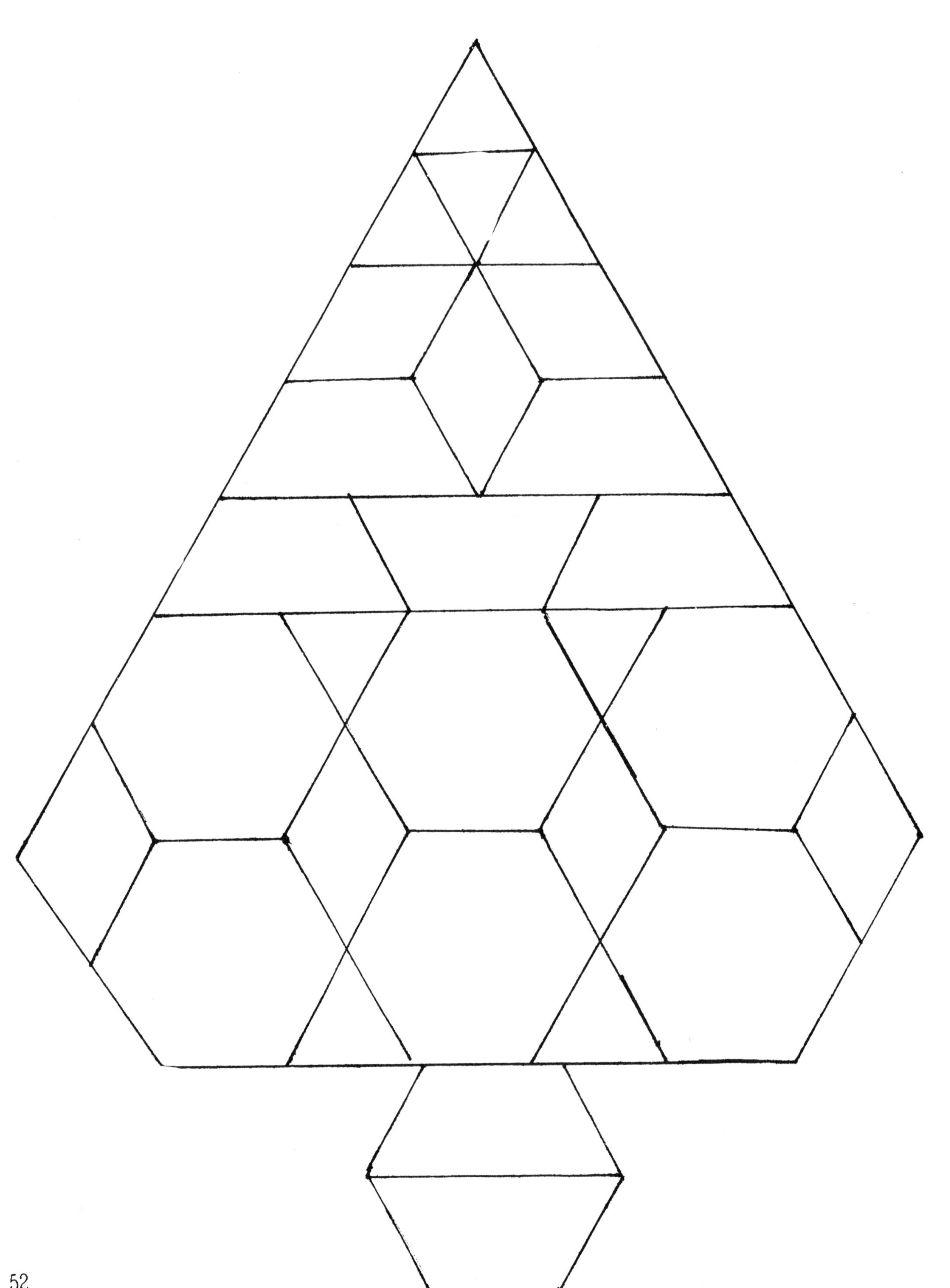

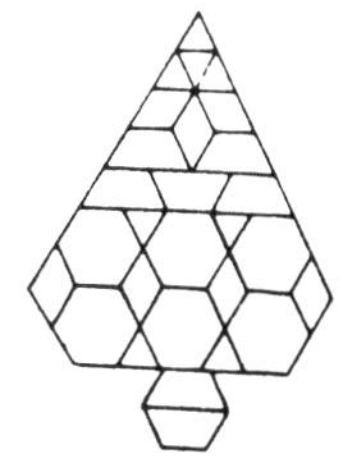

What Can You Trade for a Green Tree?

January

Grade Level: Primary

TASK ANALYSIS: 10 - Compares the size and the area of various shapes

MATERIALS: Xeroxed pattern to be used by the students (one per child), one record page per child, pencils, tubs of pattern blocks

ORGANIZATION: Whole class activity
Kindergarten/primary: 20 - 40 minutes

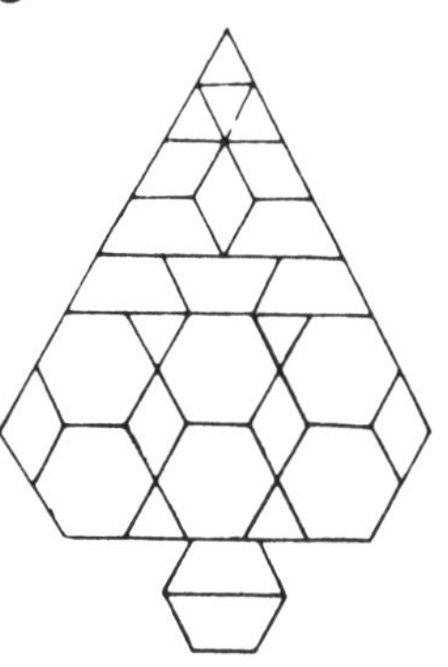

PROCEDURE:

- Give each child xeroxed pattern.
- Have child cover pattern to match the given pattern block design.
- Record the number and type of blocks used.
- Have child do a second layer using two colors of pattern blocks.
- Record data.
- Have child do a third layer using any other combination of pattern blocks and record data.
- Compare and interpret data using the following questions:
  "How many pattern blocks did you use on the first layer?"
  "How many pattern blocks did you use when you used two colors (second layer)?"
  "How many pattern blocks did you use for your combination layer?"

Compare and Exchange

Pattern	1st Layer	2nd Layer	3rd Layer

Calendar Math
February
Grade Level: Primary

TASK ANALYSIS: 1 - Locates and reads the days of the week on the calendar and is able to find given days and dates
2 - States and orders the months and the number of days in each month

MATERIALS: Calendar form (store bought lattice or made from paper or yarn),construction paper hearts, silhouettes of Lincoln and Washington (10 of each). These will be used for an AABBCC pattern, brown construction paper for large hatchet

ORGANIZATION: Whole class activity
Kindergarten/primary: 15 minutes of calendar time

  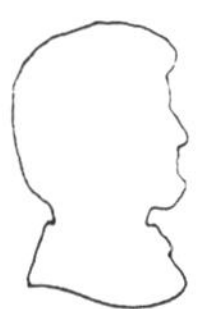   

PROCEDURE:

- Have the month, days, year, birthday gumballs, and special days on calendar at the beginning of the month.
- Put up date (alternate hats and silhouettes to form AABBCC pattern) on calendar days.
- Put daily tally mark on hatchet.
- Ask CALENDAR QUESTIONS daily.

- After a few days (as AABBCC pattern develops) ask children if they see a pattern emerging.
- Ask questions such as: "What does the calendar look like?" and "What will come next?"
- Chant the pattern together.

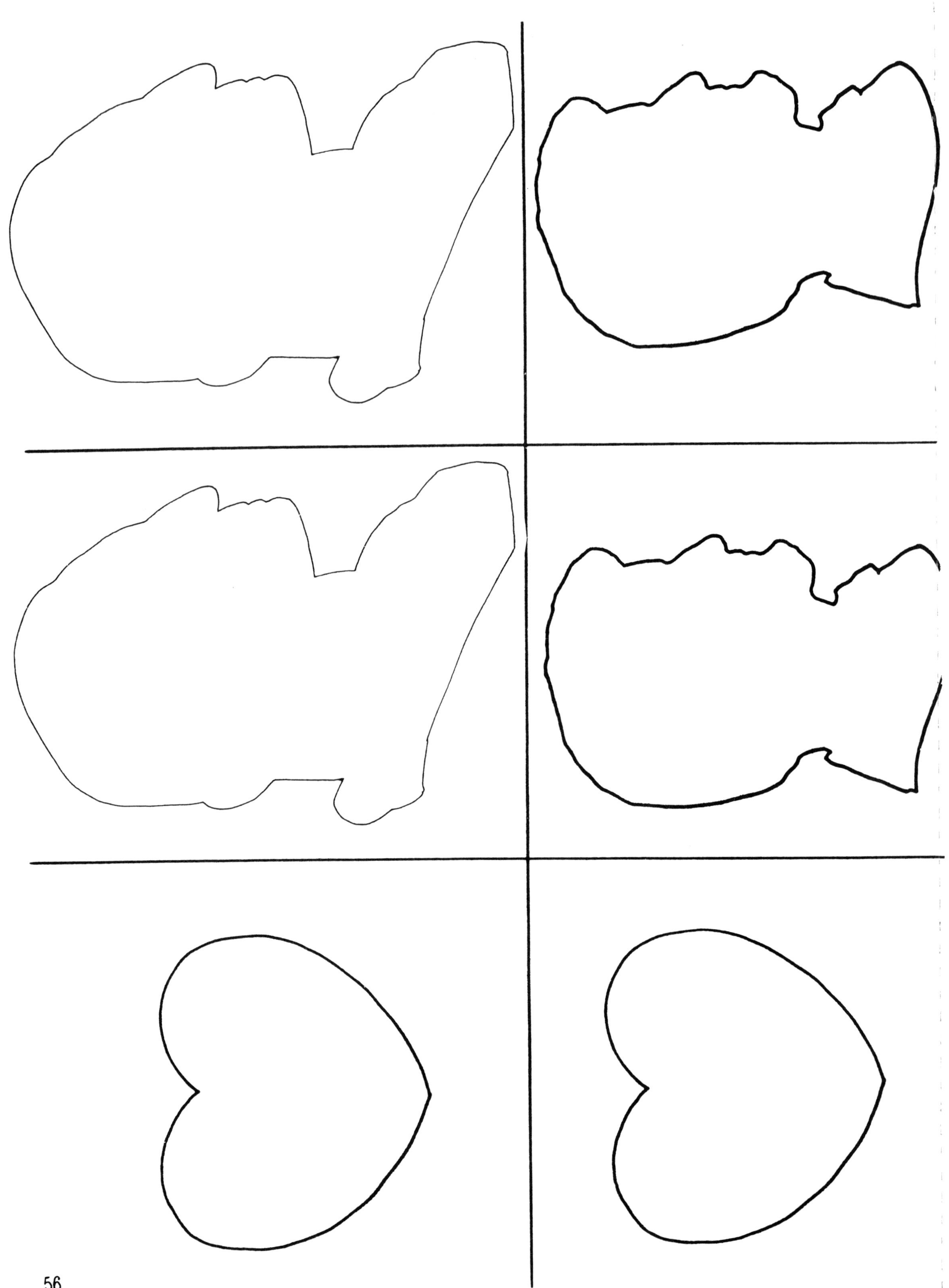

Honest Abe, What's in Your Hat?

February

Grade Level: Primary

TASK ANALYSIS: 4 - Identifies penny, nickel, and dime and states their respective value
5 - Counts to a given monetary value using coins of the same and of mixed denominations
6 - Makes change using pennies, nickels, and dimes

MATERIALS: Large stovepipe hat (teacher made or store bought), 10 small paper stovepipe hats made by students, 100 pennies, 20 nickels, 10 dimes, and 3 one dollar bills, magic wand (optional), copy of Polly, Nellie, Dorcus poem (see end of lesson).

ORGANIZATION: Whole class activity
Kindergarten/primary: 20 - 30 minutes

PROCEDURE:

- Teacher should have large stovepipe hat with 3 one dollar bills hidden inside where they can be easily reached by the teacher but not seen by the children.
- The day before the 100th day of your school year, have children (working in cooperative groups) make the 10 small stovepipe hats.
- On the 100th day have the children count ten pennies into each hat.
- In a "magical" manner, the teacher pours coins into large hat (with students counting by tens to 100).
- Everyone recites first verse of poem as teacher waves hand over the hat.
- Teacher reaches in hat during the last line of verse and pulls out a one dollar bill.

Extend the lesson by following the same procedure with the nickels (put two nickels in each of the ten small hats), count by tens as coins are put into the hats, recite second verse of poem, and withdraw a one dollar bill.
With dimes, put one coin in each hat, count by tens, recite third verse of poem, teacher withdraws 1 dollar from large hat.

Polly, Nellie, Dorcus

Polly, Nellie, Dorcus dear
100 pennies I have here.
100 pennies in my stovepipe hat
a gidget, a gadget, it comes out like that.

Polly, Nellie, Dorcus dear
20 nickels I have here.
20 nickels in my stovepipe hat
a gidget, a gadget, it comes out like that.

Polly Nellie, Dorcus dear
10 little dimes I have here.
10 little dimes in my stovepipe hat
a gidget, a gadget, it comes out like that.

Do You Have a Heavy Heart?

February

Grade Level: Primary

TASK ANALYSIS: 11 - Weighs and compares the weight of two simple objects by using arbitrary units of measure

MATERIALS: Balance-type scales for each cooperative group, tub of unifix cubes, tub of teddy bear counters, tub of pattern blocks, one recording sheet per group, 2 bags of small candy hearts (one cup of small hearts per group), (record page 50)

ORGANIZATION: Cooperative learning groups
Kindergarten/primary: 20 - 40 minutes

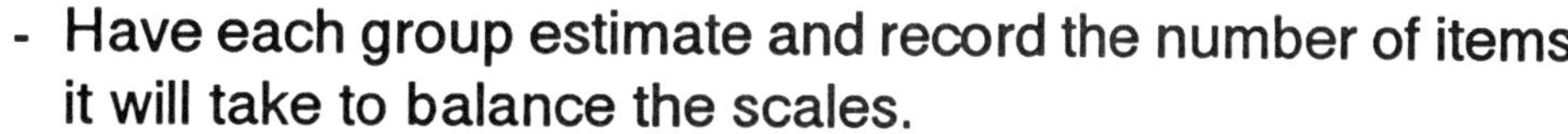

PROCEDURE:

- Each cooperative group places one cup of small hearts in scale.
- Have each group estimate and record the number of items it will take to balance the scales.
- Have each group add tub items to balance the scale.
- Count the number of items that were needed to balance.
- Ask each group to give a number sentence telling the difference between the estimate and the actual count.
- Compare and interpret data.

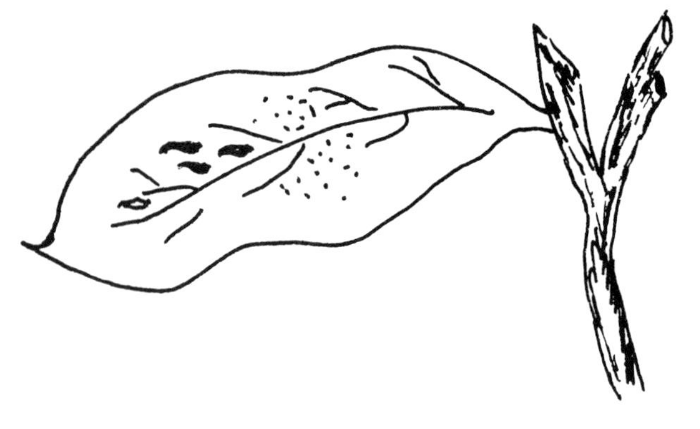

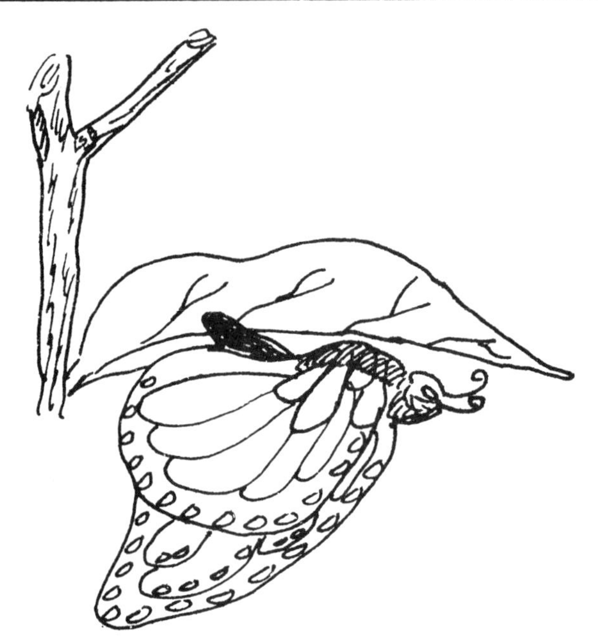

Calendar Math
March
Grade Level: Primary

TASK ANALYSIS: 1 - Locates and reads the days of the week on the calendar and is able to find given days and dates
2 - States and orders the months and the number of days in each month

MATERIALS: Calendar form (store bought lattice or made from paper or yarn), pictures or drawings of SIX stages of a butterfly (egg on leaf, caterpillar, crysallis, adult butterfly — you will need FIVE of each stage (they can be drawn by the children), construction paper for large shamrock, tally sheet

ORGANIZATION: Whole class activity
Kindergarten/primary: 15 minutes of calendar time

PROCEDURE:

- Have the month, days, year, birthday gumballs, and special days on calendar at the beginning of the month.
- Put up date (alternate the four butterfly stages) on calendar days.
- Put daily tally mark on shamrock.
- Ask CALENDAR QUESTIONS daily.

- After a few days (as ABCD pattern develops ask children if they see a pattern emerging.
- Ask questions such as: "What does the calendar look like?" and "What will come next?"
- Chant the pattern together.
- At the end of the month ask children, "How many times did the butterfly hatch?"

One Potato! Two Potato!

Items	Estimate	Actual	More or Less

One Potato! Two Potato!

March

Grade Level: Primary

TASK ANALYSIS: 11 - Weighs and compares the weight of two simple objects by using arbitrary units of measure

MATERIALS: Balance-type scales for each cooperative group, tub of unifix cubes, tub of teddy bear counters, tub of pattern blocks, one large potato per cooperative group, xerox copy of record sheet (one per group)

ORGANIZATION: Cooperative learning groups
Kindergarten/primary: 20-40 minutes

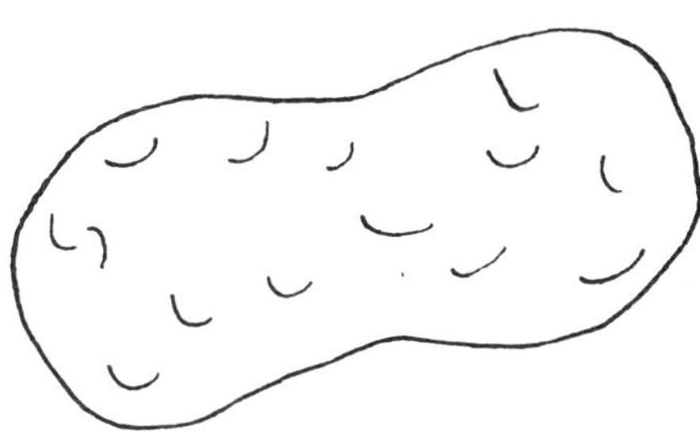

PROCEDURE:

- Each cooperative group places potato in scale.
- Have each group estimate and record the number of tub items it will take to balance the scales.
- Have each group add items to make the scale balance.
- Count and record the number of items that were needed to balance.
- Ask each group to give a number sentence telling the difference between the estimate and the actual count.
- Compare and interpret data.

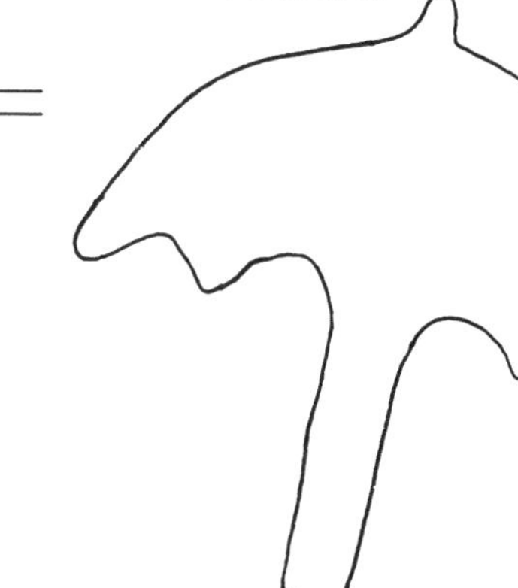

Calendar Math

April

Grade Level: Primary

TASK ANALYSIS: 1 - Locates and reads the days of the week on the calendar and is able to find given days and dates
2 - States and orders the months and the number of days in each month

MATERIALS: Calendar form (store bought lattice or made from paper or yarn), construction paper umbrellas made of six different colors (to form an ABCDEF pattern), blue construction paper for large raindrop (tally sheet).

ORGANIZATION: Whole class activity
Kindergarten/primary: 15 minutes of calendar time

PROCEDURE:

- Have the month, days, year, birthday gumballs, and special days on calendar at the beginning of the month.
- Put up date (alternate colored umbrellas to form ABCDEF pattern) on calendar days.
- Put daily tally mark on raindrop.
- Ask CALENDAR QUESTIONS daily.

- After a few days (as ABCDEF pattern develops ask children if they see a pattern emerging.
- Have children predict the color of the next umbrella each day.
- "How many different ways can you see the pattern?"
- At the end of the month, tally the number of times the pattern has been repeated.

3:00	2:15
9:30	12:00
8:45	10:15

Clancy Clock

April

Grade Level: Primary

TASK ANALYSIS: 3 - Identifies hour and minute (hands/symbols) on both a standard and digital clock and is able to set time to the hour, half-hour, and quarter hour

MATERIALS: Large Clancy Clock and materials for students to make their own desk size clocks if they did not make one in the winter clock lesson (pages 48-49), 10 to 15 feet of clothesline rope to make a large circle on the floor or ground, clock flash-cards.

ORGANIZATION: Whole class activity
Kindergarten/primary: 20 - 30 minutes

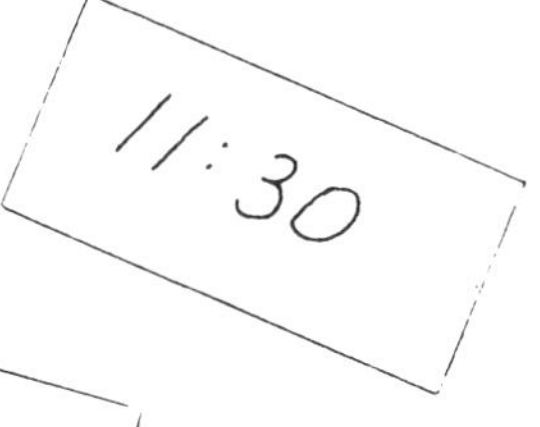

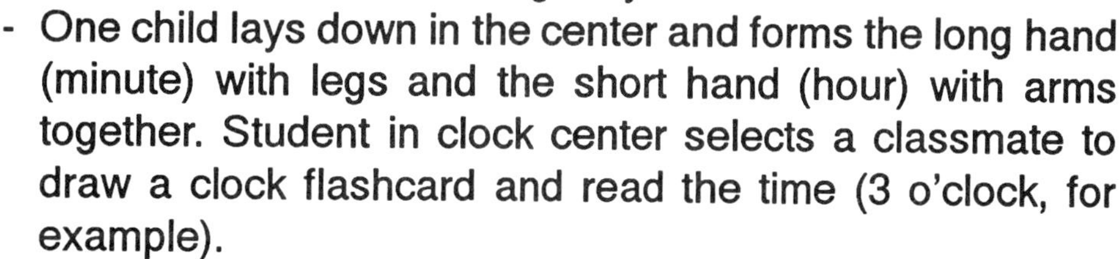

PROCEDURE:

- Teacher and/or children make flashcards beforehand.
- Lay clothesline on floor to form a clock circle.
- One child sits at each imaginary clock number.
- One child lays down in the center and forms the long hand (minute) with legs and the short hand (hour) with arms together. Student in clock center selects a classmate to draw a clock flashcard and read the time (3 o'clock, for example).
- Student in center then demonstrates the time with arms and legs.
- The "hour hand" child (student who is sitting at 3 o'clock then becomes the center child.
- Center child selects a classmate to fill the 3 o'clock spot.
- Rotate until every child has a chance to participate.

4:00

6:30

1:00

8:15

7:45

11:30

Spring Shopping Spree

April

Grade Level: Primary

TASK ANALYSIS: 4 - Identifies penny, nickel, and dime and states their respective value
5 - Counts to a given monetary value using coins of the same and of mixed denominations
6 - Makes change using pennies, nickels, andd dimes

MATERIALS: Sheet of coins (pennies, nickels, dimes), tape, open boxes of small items for children to "purchase" (merchandise should be classroom items which children use for the math period or for the day), 3 small coin boxes, scissors

ORGANIZATION: Whole class activity (done in cooperative groups)
Kindergarten/primary: 20 - 30 minutes

PROCEDURE:

- Teacher tapes paper coins to desks, chairs, tables, closets, books, etc. before children arrive.
- Give each child a sheet of coins to cut out.
- Explain monetary value of each box of merchandise.
- Exact change must be used to purchase an item.
- Throughout the day, as children find taped coins, they may do the following:

  Describe to a classmate the coin;s name and value.

  Go on a shopping spree to purchase from correct merchandise box.
- During math time, children may share number sentences about the shopping spree.

Umbrella

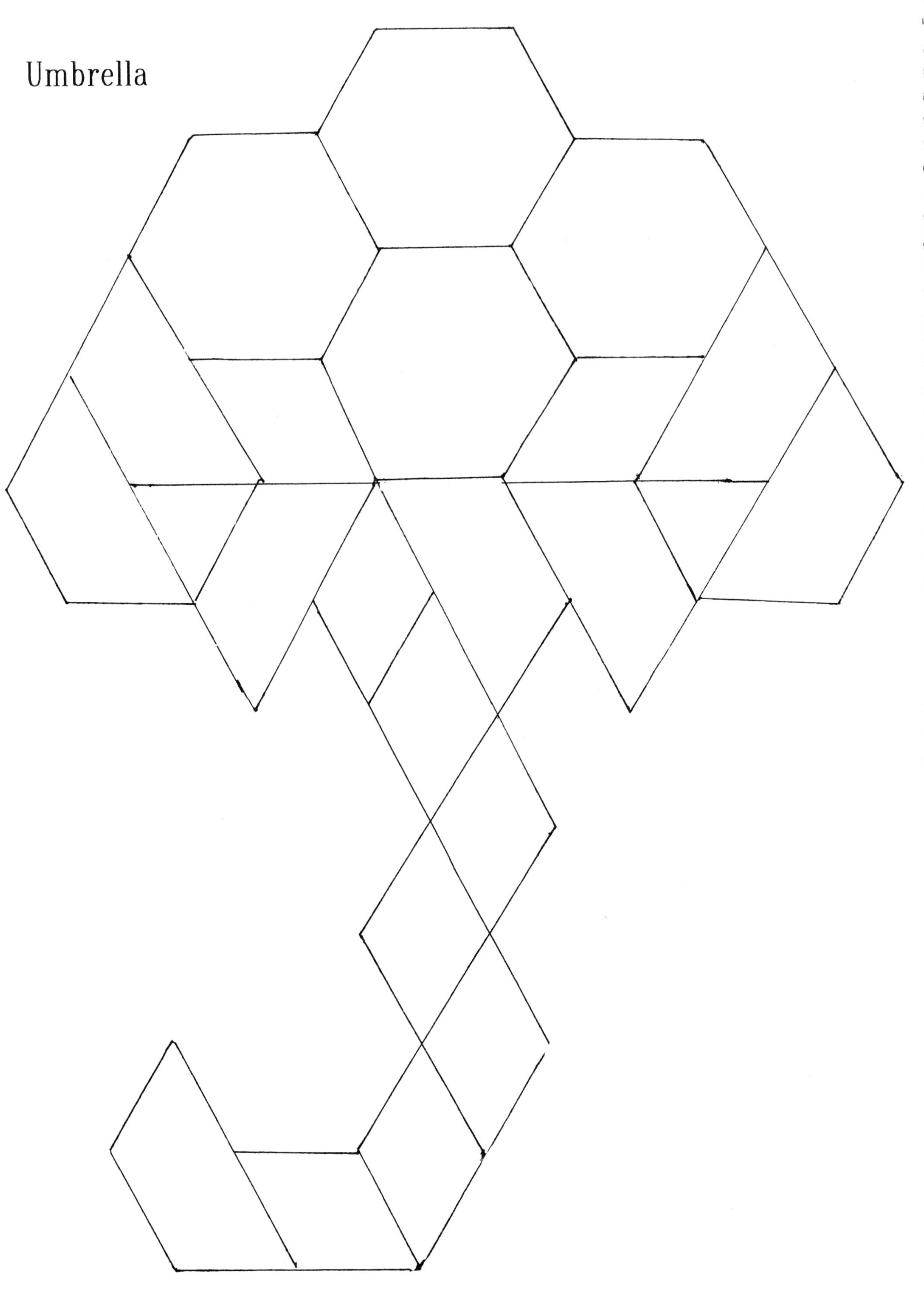

Umbrella and Bunny Mix 'N' Match

April

Grade Level: Primary

TASK ANALYSIS: 10 - Compares size and area of various shapes

MATERIALS: Xeroxed patterns to be used by the children, one record sheet (page 82) per child, pencils, tubs of pattern blocks

ORGANIZATION: Whole class activity
Kindergarten/primary: 20 - 40 minutes

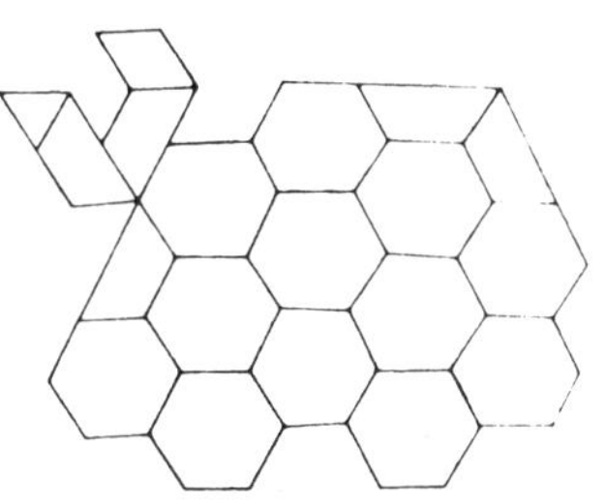

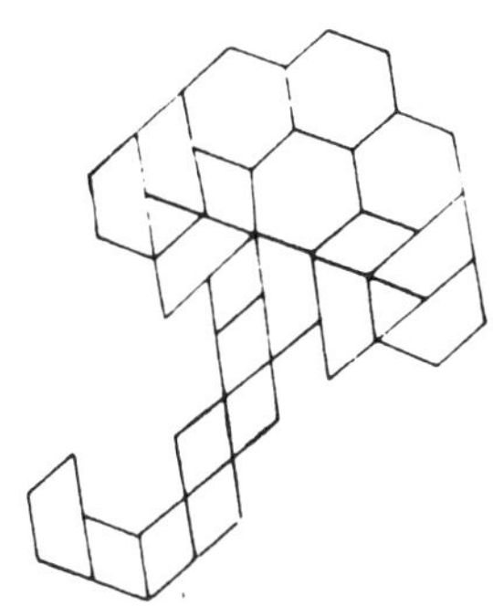

PROCEDURE:

- Give each child xeroxed pattern.
- Have child cover pattern to match the given pattern block design.
- Record the number and type of blocks used.
- Have child do a second layer using two colors of pattern blocks.
- Record data.
- Have child do a third layer using any other combination of pattern blocks and record data.
- Compare and interpret data using the following questions:
- "How many pattern blocks did you use when you used two colors (second layer)?"
- "How many pattern blocks did you use for your combination layer?"

Bunny

Hot Roasted Peanuts!

April

Grade Level: Primary

TASK ANALYSIS: 11 - Weighs and compares the weight of two simple objects by using arbitrary units of measure

MATERIALS: Balance-type scales for each cooperative group, tub of unifix cubes, tub of teddy bear counters, tub of pattern blocks, etc., one recording sheet per group, 2 large jars of roasted peanuts (two cups per cooperative group)

ORGANIZATION: Cooperative learning groups
Kindergarten/primary: 20-40 minutes

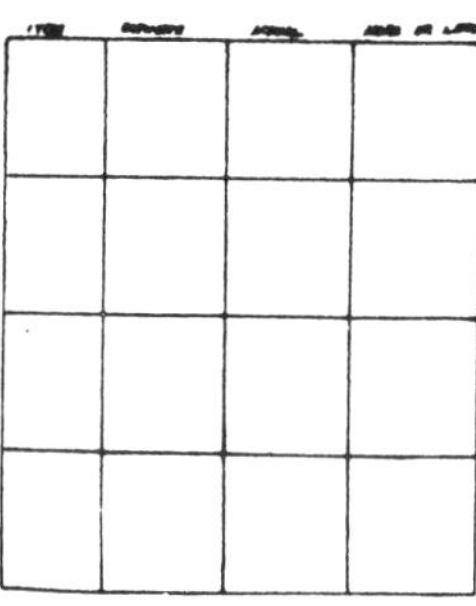

PROCEDURE:
- Each cooperative group places peanuts in scale.
- Each group estimates and records the number of items needed to balance the scales.
- Have each group add items to balance the scale.
- Count the number of tub items used to balance.
- Ask each group to give a number sentence telling the difference between the estimate and actual count.
- Compare and interpret data.

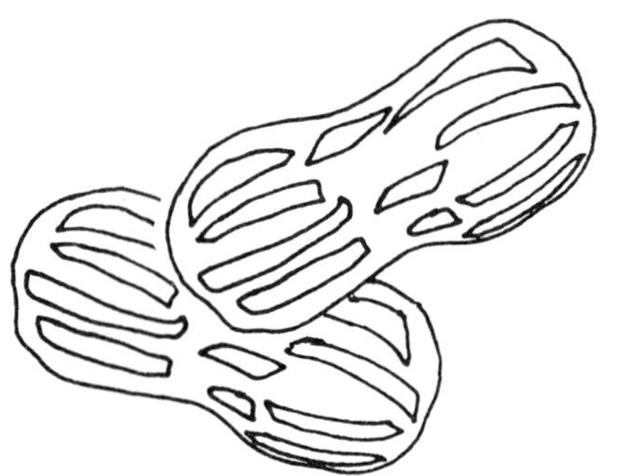

Hot Roasted Peanuts!

Items	Estimate	Actual	More or Less

Calendar Math

May

Grade Level: Primary

TASK ANALYSIS: 1 - Locates and reads the days of the week on the calendar and is able to find given days and dates
2 - States and orders the months and the number of days in each month

MATERIALS: Calendar form (store bought lattice or made from paper or yarn), construction paper flowers (daisy, tulip, and daffodil) which the children can make, construction paper for large tulip (with stem and leaves)

ORGANIZATION: Whole class activity
Kindergarten/primary: 15 minutes of calendar time

PROCEDURE:

- Have the month, days, year, birthday gumballs, and special days on calendar at the beginning of the month.
- Put up date and have the children predict what flower will come up next (alternate the three flower types to form ABC pattern) on calendar days.
- Put daily tally mark on tulip.
- Ask CALENDAR QUESTIONS daily.

- After a few days (as ABC pattern develops) ask children if they see a pattern emerging.
- Ask questions such as: "What does the calendar look like?" and "What will come next?"
- Chant the pattern together.
- Tally the pattern throughout the month to help children see how many times it has been repeated.

Piggy Bank

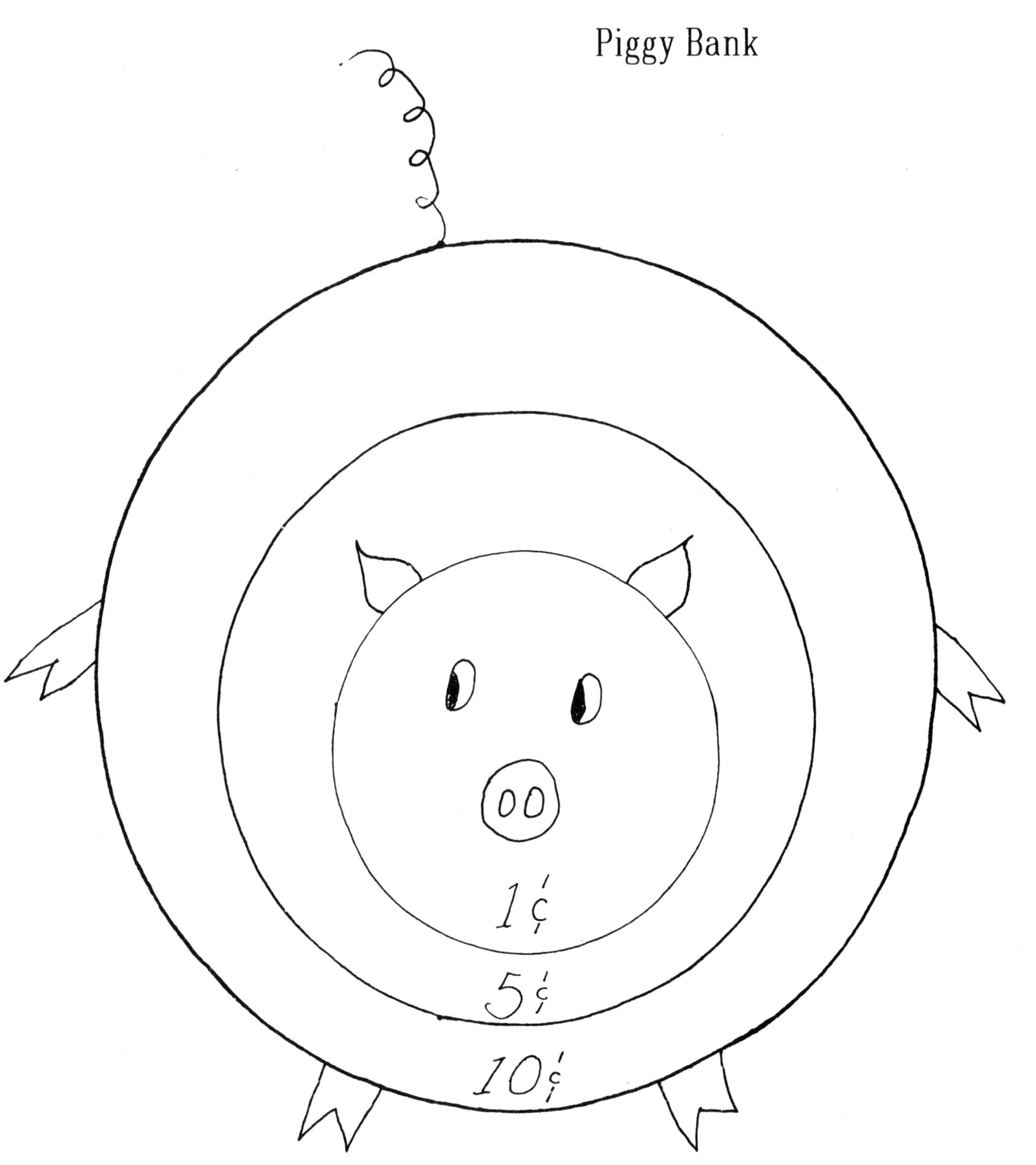

What Coins Are in Your Piggy Bank?

May

Grade Level: Primary

TASK ANALYSIS: 4 - Identifies penny, nickel, and dime and states their respective value
5 - Counts to a given monetary value using coins of the same and of mexed denominations
6 - Makes change using pennies, nickels, andd dimes

MATERIALS: Sheet of coins (pennies, nickels, dimes — page 14), scissors, index card flashcards with money amounts on them (i.e. 20 cents), piggy bank diagram project

ORGANIZATION: Whole class activity
Kindergarten/primary: 20 - 30 minutes

PROCEDURE:

- Teacher makes money flashcards.
- Teacher gives children coin sheets to cut out coins and sheet of piggy bank diagram project.
- After completing the piggy bank project, teacher models flashcard procedure.
- Take flashcard and show children the amount (i.e. 20 cents).
- One child specifies what coins will be placed in piggy banks to equal that amount.
- All children place like coins in their banks.
- Do this for five flashcards and then have children give number sentences telling how many pennies, nickels, and dimes they have in their piggy banks. All children should have the same number of each coin.
- Empty piggy banks.
- Take flashcard and show children the amount.
- Have children fill piggy bank with most coins, least coins, and other combinations of coins. Record.
- Children give number sentences to compare data.

Butterfly

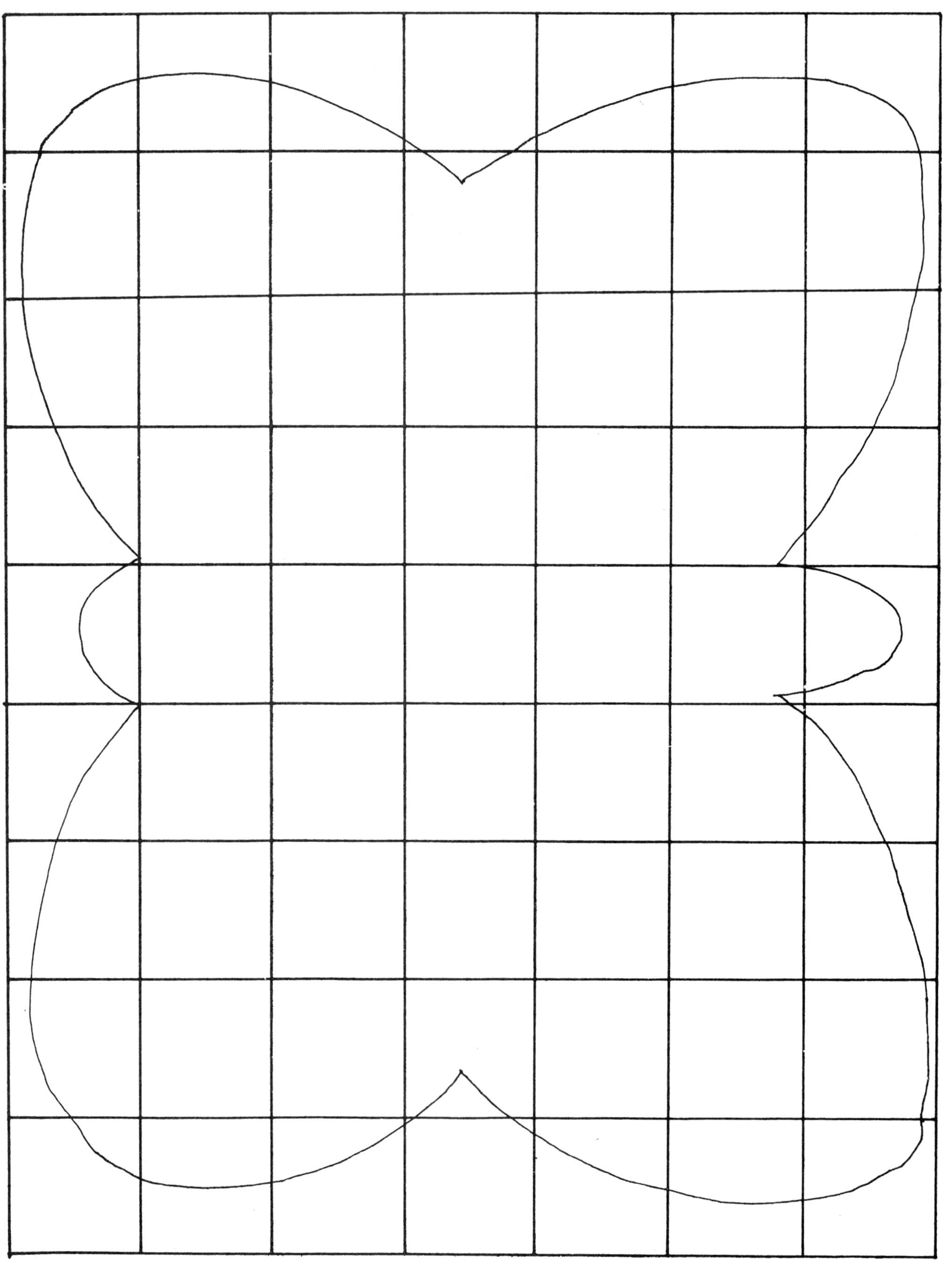

Estimate ______ Actual ______

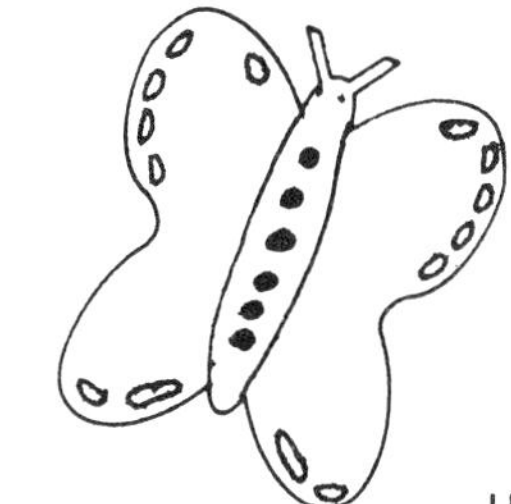

Butterfly and Easter Egg Squared

May

Grade Level: Primary

TASK ANALYSIS: 9 - Builds and counts the number of square units inside a figure

MATERIALS: Xeroxed grid page 24 (one per pair), 1 inch tiles, xeroxed patterns (one per pair)

ORGANIZATION: Whole class activity with students working in cooperative groups of two.
Kindergarten/primary: 20 - 30 minutes

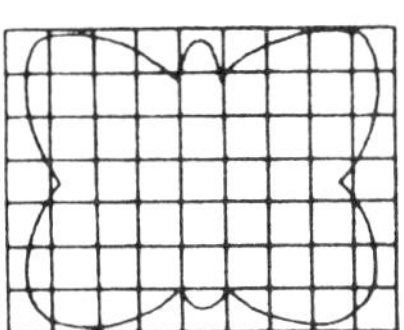

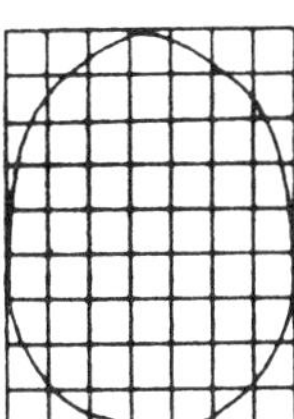

PROCEDURE:

- Give each group two xeroxed patterns, one grid page and tub of inch tiles.
- Ask groups to estimate the number of tiles it will take to cover the patterns.
- Record estimate.
- Have the children cover the pattern with the tiles.
- Count and record the number of tiles used.
- Compare and estimate the actual count.
- Have children choose an object to trace on the grid page.
- Estimate and record the number of tiles needed to cover the pattern.
- Have children cover the pattern with tiles.
- Count and record the number of tiles used.
- Discuss estimate and actual count.

Easter Egg

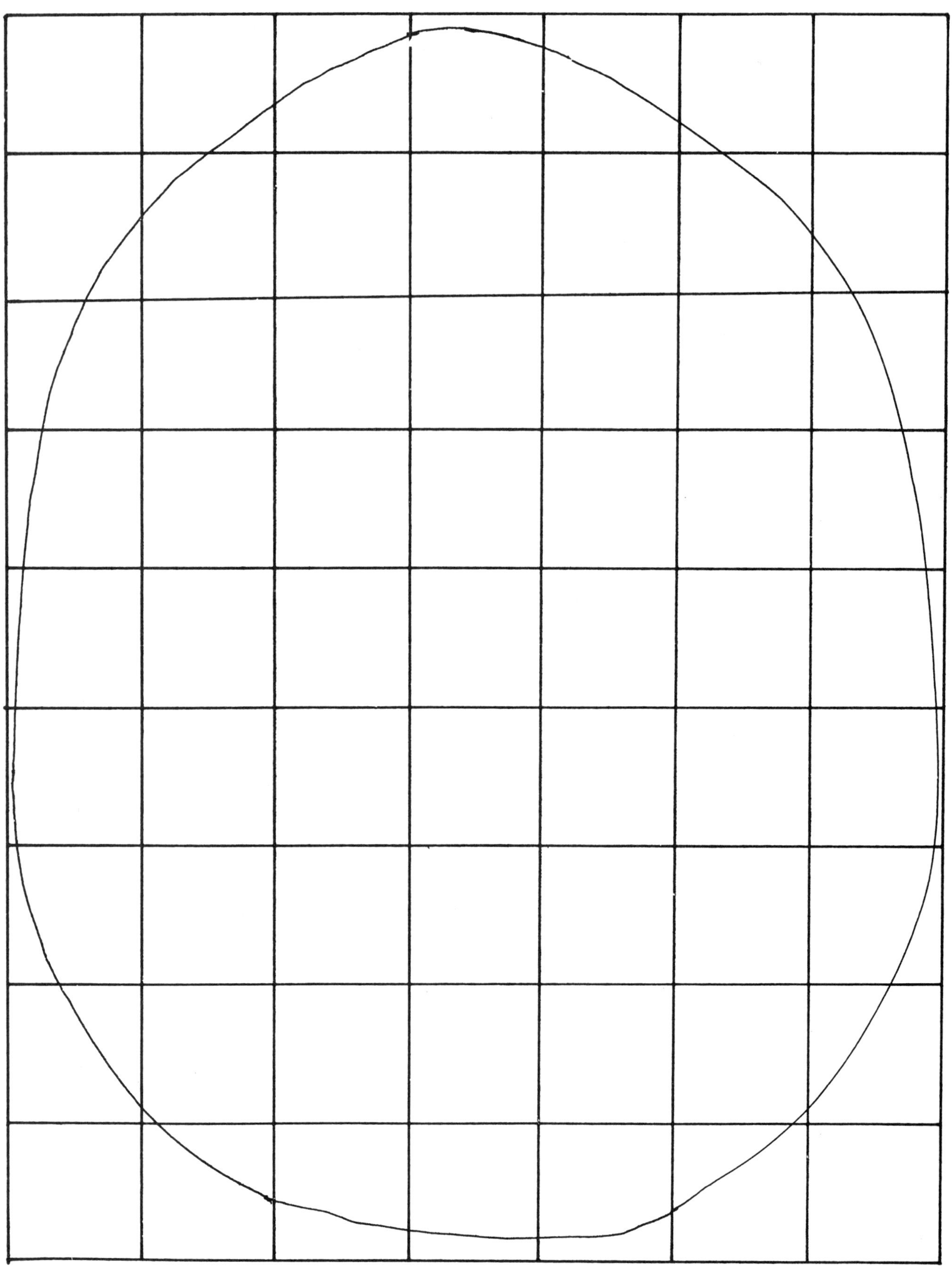

Estimate ______ Actual ______

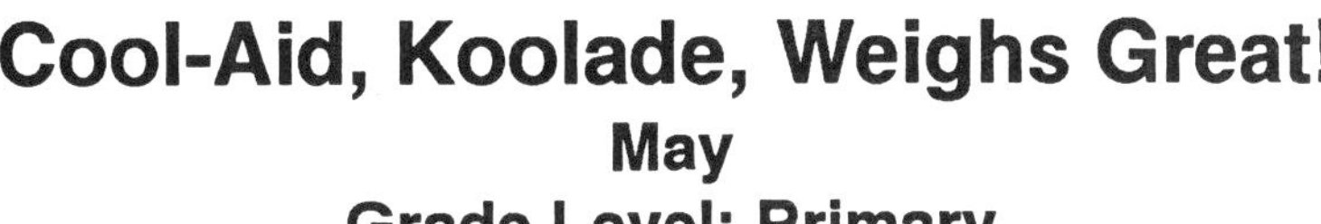

Cool-Aid, Koolade, Weighs Great!

May

Grade Level: Primary

TASK ANALYSIS: 12 - Uses Arbitrary units to make an estimate, a measurement, and order for the volume of various containers

MATERIALS: Several packages of Koolade drink mix, various sized containers (film canisters, small mustard jars, baby food jars, etc.), clear plastic drinking cups with children's names written on them, marking pen

ORGANIZATION: Cooperative learning groups
Kindergarten/primary: 20 - 40 minutes

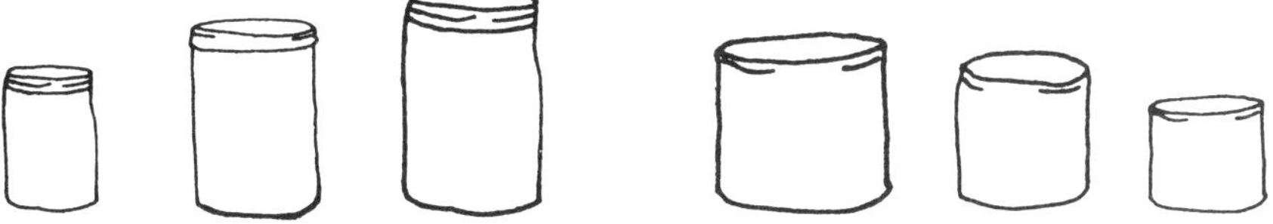

PROCEDURE:

- As a whole group, have children predict what jar will be needed to hold enough juice for the whole class.
- Divide into cooperative groups.
- Have each group prepare Koolade mix.
- Have each group do a second estimate of the size of jars needed.
- Have each group measure the Koolade mix by experimenting with various jars.
- As a whole class, have students line up the various jars in order of volume (least to greatest, greatest to least).
- Let children choose their favorite arbitrary unit amount.
- Measure that amount into each drinking cup and compare with classmates to let children see the need for standard units.
- Decide as a class on the unit they all want for a drink.
- Fill their cups and enjoy!

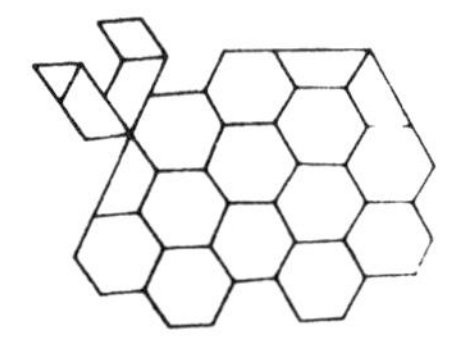

Compare and Exchange

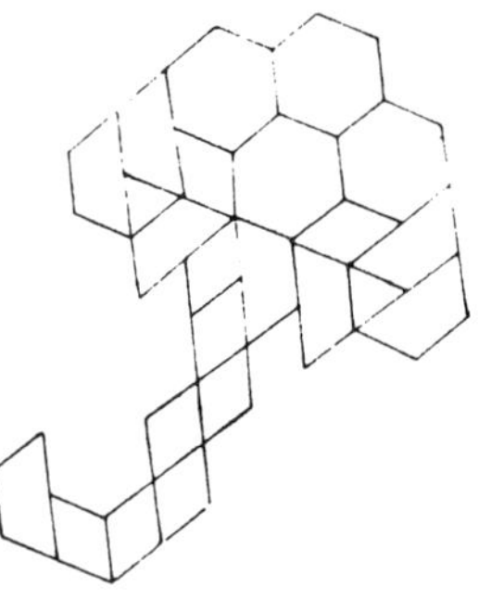

Pattern	1st Layer	2nd Layer	3rd Layer

Lemonade Stand, What's Your Volume?

May

Grade Level: Primary

TASK ANALYSIS: 13 - Measures amounts in pints, quarts, and gallons

MATERIALS: Jugs, various sized jars, sugar, lemons (brought by children), ladles, spoons, cups, juicer, strainer, pint, quart, and gallon containers

ORGANIZATION: Cooperative learning groups
Kindergarten/primary: 20 - 30 minutes

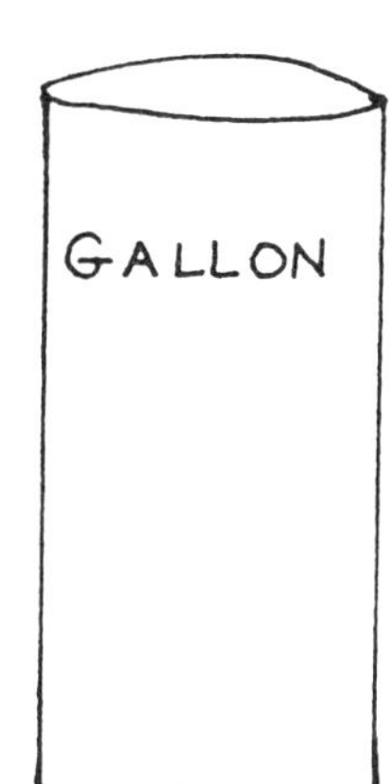

PROCEDURE:

- Discuss the attributes of lemons: color, taste, texture.
- Compare and discuss the likes and differences of the lemons brought by the children.
- Questions to be asked:
  "What will the juice taste like?"
  "Will there be more juice from this lemon than that lemon?"
- Children estimate how many pints, quarts, and gallons of juice can be make from all the lemons.
- "How many drinking cups will each pint fill?'
- Give each group the materials and ingredients needed to make lemonade.
- Ask the children to divide the juice equally within their own groups.
- Drink the juice.

Rainbow Cards

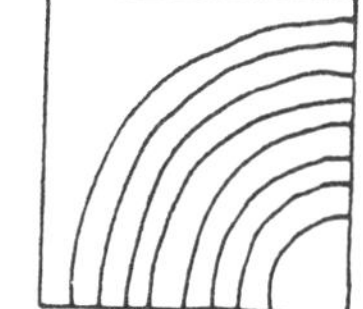

Calendar Math

June

Grade Level: Primary

TASK ANALYSIS: 1 - Locates and reads the days of the week on the calendar and is able to find given days and dates
2 - States and orders the months and the number of days in each month

MATERIALS: Calendar form (store bought lattice or made from paper or yarn), drawings of the rainbow on square cards that will fill your calendar lattice; the first card has a red arch, second card has red and orange arches, third card has red, orange, and yellow, fourth card has red, orange, yellow, and green arches, fifth card has red, orange, yellow, green, and blue, sixth card has same five colors plus indigo, and for the seventh card add violet to the first six colors. Make enough cards for the entire month, construction paper to make ladybug for daily tally

ORGANIZATION: Whole class activity
Kindergarten/primary: 15 minutes of calendar time

PROCEDURE:

- Have the month, days, year, birthday gumballs, and special days on calendar at the beginning of the month.
- Put up date (rainbow cards form patterns both diagonally and horizontally) on calendar days.
- Put daily tally mark on ladybug.
- Ask CALENDAR QUESTIONS daily.

- After a few days (as rainbow pattern develops) ask children if they see a pattern emerging.
- Ask questions such as: "What does the calendar look like?" and "What will come next?"
- Chant the pattern together.

Safety

PITCH IN
SCHOOL BUS STOP AHEAD
FIRE EXTINGUISHER
RESTROOMS
INFORMATION
PLAYGROUND
WOMEN
NO BICYCLES
FIRST AID
MEN
PELIGRO
NO ENTRE
DANGER
DO NOT ENTER
TELEPHONE

Calendar Math

June

Grade Level: Primary

TASK ANALYSIS: 1 - Locates and reads the days of the week on the calendar and is able to find given days and dates
2 - States and orders the months and the number of days in each month

MATERIALS: Calendar form (store bought lattice or made from paper or yarn), pictures of safety signs (stop, go, don't walk, bike lane, and others pertinent to your locale)

ORGANIZATION: Whole class activity
Kindergarten/primary: 15 minutes of calendar time

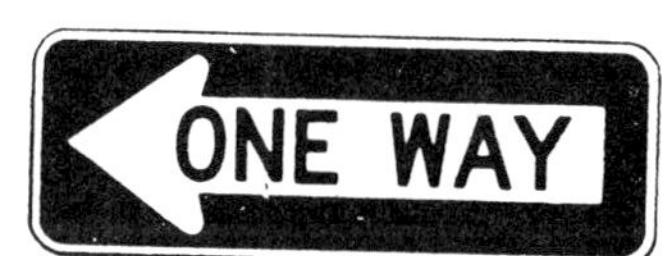

PROCEDURE:

- Have the month, days, year, birthday gumballs, and special days on calendar at the beginning of the month.
- Put up date (alternate various signs to form AABBCC pattern) on calendar days.
- Put daily tally mark on calendar.
- Ask CALENDAR QUESTIONS daily.

- After a few days (as AABBCC pattern develops) ask children if they see a pattern emerging.
- Ask questions such as: "What does the calendar look like?" and "What will come next?"
- Chant the pattern together.

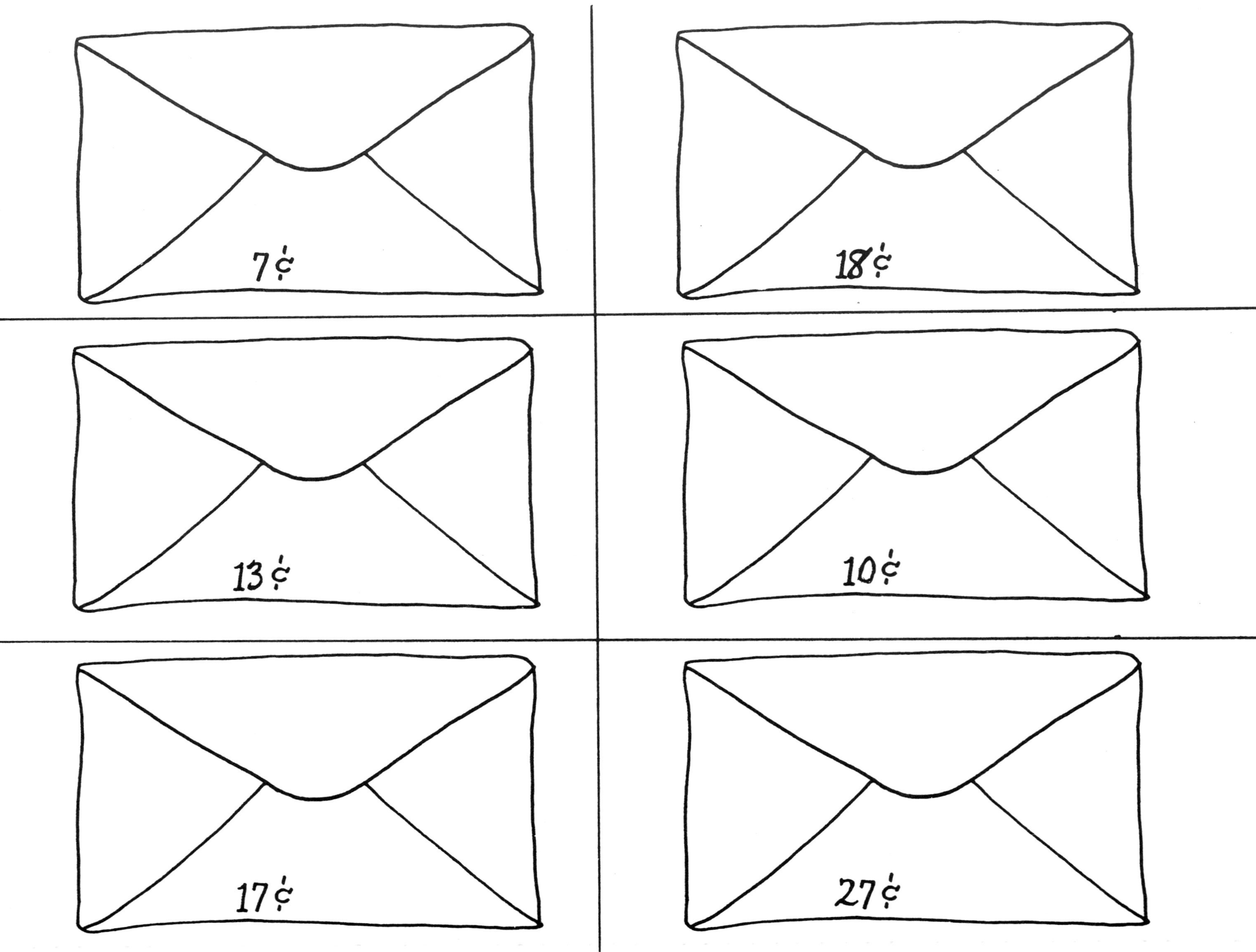
7¢
18¢
13¢
10¢
17¢
27¢

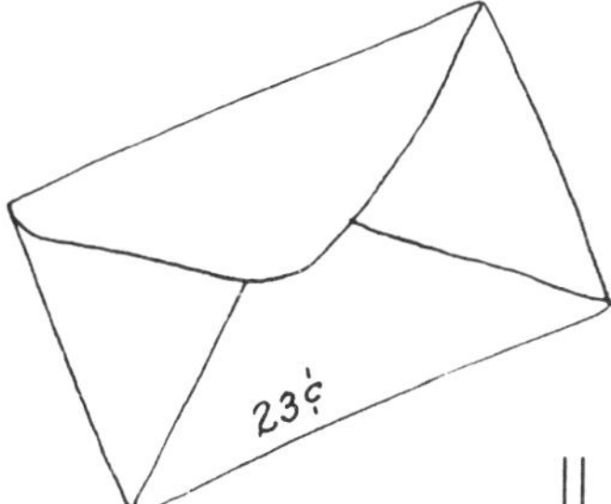

Rainbow Shopping

June

Grade Level: Primary

TASK ANALYSIS: 4 - Identifies penny, nickel, and dime and states their respective value
5 - Counts to a given monetary value using coins of the same and of mexed denominations
6 - Makes change using pennies, nickels, andd dimes

MATERIALS: Envelopes with the amount enclosed shown on the outside, sheet of coins (pennies, nickels, dimes), marking pens, merchandise boxes covered with seven colors of the rainbow (merchandise used should be classroom items that the child is "purchasing" for the math period or the day), colored 2 x 3 construction paper "tickets," scissors

ORGANIZATION: Whole class activity
Kindergarten/primary: 20 - 30 minutes

PROCEDURE:

- There are two steps which the teacher must complete in preparation for this lesson. First, cover seven boxes with paper (red, orange, yellow, green, blue, indigo, violet) and label each box with a specific value (1,5,10,15,20,25,30 cents). Second, make rainbow shopping envelopes (three per student) by placing a colored ticket in an envelope and writing a monetary amount on the outside of the envelope.
- Amounts must be greater than the value of the given rainbow box (i.e. if red box is 5 cents, all red ticketed envelopes must be 5 cents or more).
- Give each child an envelope.
- Have child fill it with real coins.
- Give each child a sheet of coins to cut out (these will be used for recording and self-checking).

- Select seven storekeepers.
- Children begin shopping -- purchasing an item from their rainbow color.
- Children show storekeeper their envelopes and choose an item; storekeeper writes amount on their envelope and storekeeper makes change.

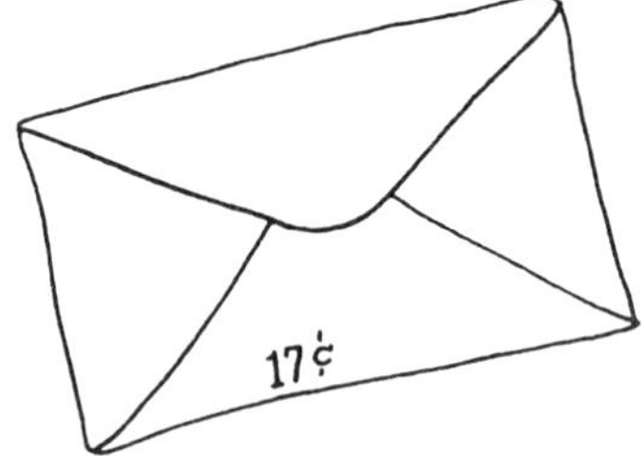

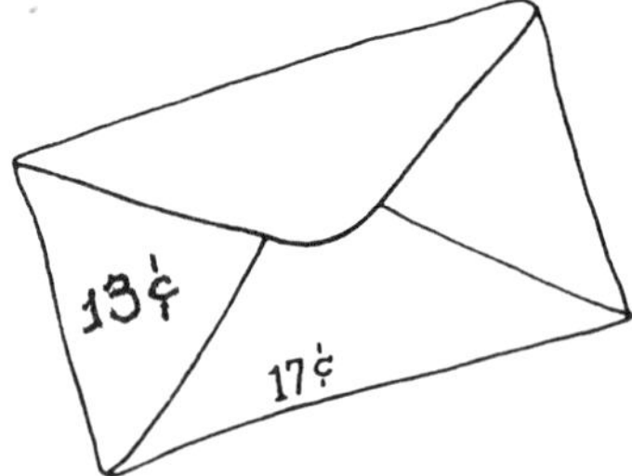

- Children take purchased items, envelopes and remaining money to their seats.
- Children share with a classmate their rainbow shopping spree using their paper coins.

Rainbow envelope:    

Cost of item purchased: 13¢ Amount paid:  

Change from storekeeper:  

Total of money left:    

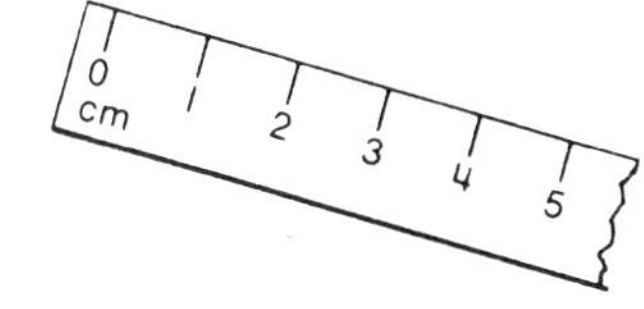

Buttons, Bows, and Arrows, With What Shall I Measure?

June

Grade Level: Primary

TASK ANALYSIS: 8 - Estimates and counts units of length and establishes need for standard units of measure

MATERIALS: Measuring tools for inch, foot, and yard; items gathered in the classroom and items brought from home which students can measure (bats, rods, canes, golf clubs, arrows, hair ribbons, shoes, belts, etc.), several non-standard units of measure for children to explore (paper clips, pencils, crayons, watches, cuisinaire rods, etc.), butcher paper, marking pens

ORGANIZATION: Whole class activity with children working in cooperative groups of two
Kindergarten/primary: 20 - 30 minutes

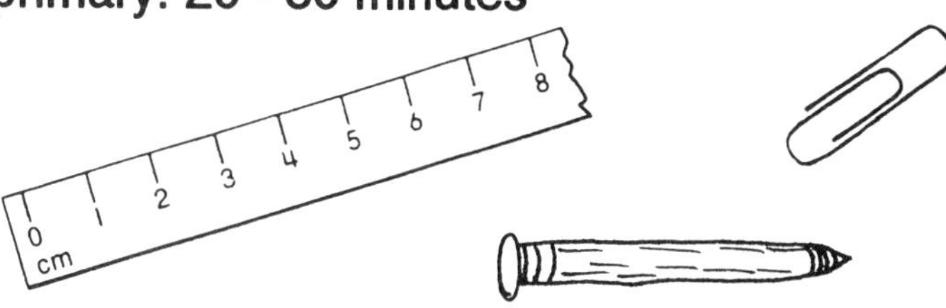

PROCEDURE:

- Choose one item and have children estimate the number it will take to measure the length.
- Record estimates on butcher paper.
- Have children use the unit chosen to measure the length.
- Count the number of units used (or needed) and record actual count on butcher paper.
- Repeat this procedure using different units of measure (standard and non-standard).
- Measure at least ten different items with arbitrary units of measure and then compare.
- Record all data on chart.
- Compare and discuss need for standard unit of measure.

Juicy, Jumpy Jelly Beans!

Items	Estimate	Actual	More or Less

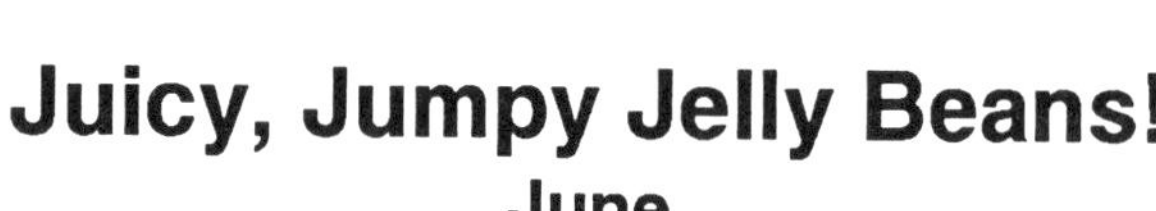

Juicy, Jumpy Jelly Beans!

June

Grade Level: Primary

TASK ANALYSIS: 11 - Weighs and compares the weight of two simple objects by using arbitrary units of measure

MATERIALS: Balance-type scales for each cooperative group, tub of unifix cubes, tub of teddy bear counters, tub of pattern blocks, one recording sheet per group, 3 bags of jelly beans (two cups per group)

ORGANIZATION: Cooperative learning groups
Kindergarten/primary: 20 - 40 minutes

PROCEDURE:

- Each cooperative group places jelly beans in scale.
- Have each group estimate and record the number of tub items it will take to balance the scales.
- Have each group add tub items to balance the scale.
- Count and record the number of items that were needed to balance the scale.
- Ask each group to give a number sentence telling the difference between the estimate and the actual count.